ten poems

to say

goodbye

also by roger housden

ten poems

to say

goodbye

ROGER HOUSDEN

HARMONY BOOKS
NEW YORK

Library of Congress Cataloging-in-Publication Data
is available upon request.

ISBN 978-0-307-88599-9
eISBN 978-0-307-88601-9

Printed in the United States of America

Book series design by Karen Minster
Jacket design by Nupoor Gordon
Jacket photographs: (windowsill) © Robert Jones/Arcangel Images,
(bowl with petals) © Kate Sears/Getty Images
Author photograph: DavidMullerPhotography.com

10 9 8 7 6 5 4 3 2 1

First Edition

contents

That's how we live,
*   always*
saying goodbye.

—Rilke, 8th *Duino Elegy*

And yet . . .

How does an essence of the world
Leave the world?
How does wetness leave water?
Don't even try.
You are here to stay.

—Rumi

introduction

I sit here in the gathering afternoon of my life and already, on the horizon, I can glimpse the golden shadows of the end of time. My own time. They cast their glow even on this present moment, sitting here with the whole of San Francisco Bay glistening blue before me. For as I feel and know more deeply the passing nature of all things, all moments, all loves and sorrows, and especially of myself and all that I hold dear, the moments that remain to me, starting with this one, take on a deeper texture and reality.

In earlier years, when my sun was nearer noon, a moment was obscured all too easily by the endless rush of moments coming after it. There was a whole life left to live, with the best surely still to come. So much of my life has been lived not at the time of the living itself, but only afterward or in anticipation, which is to say partially. So many moments were left unrecognized for what they were— my life streaming in and over me in the shape of the only sensations I would ever know at the time, irreplaceable.

Especially when those sensations were painful, pregnant with sorrow and loss, it was all too tempting to move on to the next thing, the next person, the next event. In the name of detachment, that old Buddhist virtue, I might have said; though in reality I was only trying to protect myself from the feeling of hurt. Joy, and love of course, can invite the opposite reaction to pain: the urge to hold on, not wanting to let the precious feeling go.

But the fullness of life escapes us either way, whether we are holding on or pushing away, I realize now, at this late hour. For at the heart of love is openness. An unfettered openness of heart and spirit, it seems to me, is what intimacy—with another and with all life—really means. That openness is what I now believe true detachment to be.

We let everything in and through, willing to feel more rather than less, even if it rocks our very foundations. Easy to say, not so easy to do. But we have a lifetime to practice, and it's never too late. I know now, late in my day but not too late, to "catch the winged moment as it flies," to paraphrase William Blake. Better to feel the fullness of the experience even as it is leaving, which it always must, rather than nurture regrets for months, perhaps years afterward for what could have been said, or felt, but was not.

Catching the winged moment as it flies is, I believe, a true hello and goodbye all in one: a wholehearted embrace of the way life is showing up for us now, even as we acknowledge and, yes, even wave at its leaving. And because I know I do not always live like this, caught as I sometimes am in the holding on or the pushing away, I turn to poetry to help me in the moments of my need. Poetry reminds me of what I know and often forget. Poetry speaks for me what my own tongue sometimes cannot. Poetry can coax from the shadows of my heart those feelings whose existence I may even have been afraid to admit to.

We have to say goodbye to everything eventually, and life is punctuated with a thousand goodbyes, some greater, some smaller, all along the way. And yet all too often, we can't find the words to say goodbye. We may leave a relationship or see a loved one die without ever being able to find the words or the courage to express feelings that have moved like weather in us for years. We can be at a loss for what to say when a relationship ends, when our friend or lover dies, when we wake up one morning and realize that a whole period of our life—our youth, our career, our healthy body, perhaps—is no longer what it was.

This is precisely where poetry shines. Good poetry is not merely a few thoughtful words to fill in an awkward moment. It is not simply sage advice or a gentle consolation. No, great poetry reaches down into the depths of our humanity and captures the very essence of our experience. Then it delivers it up in exactly the right words. This is why we shudder with recognition when we hear the right poem at the right time.

I have felt that shudder myself more than once in these last few years. I have attended my mother's funeral, lost a dear friend, ended a marriage, and left a city that I had grown to love.

When my marriage ended, I read my wife "The God Abandons Anthony," the astonishing poem by the Greek poet Cavafy. Anthony and Cleopatra are about to lose the city of Alexandria to the Roman army. Anthony is also losing the protection of Dionysus, god of music and wine. He stands on a balcony as a procession of musicians walks by. The poet urges him not to turn away from the beauty of the music, but to turn toward it; to take in the full impact of the loss he is going to sustain; to be willing to listen

> To the exquisite music of that strange procession,
> And say goodbye to her, to the Alexandria you
>   are leaving.[1]

Can we stand to gaze into the heart of our loss, the preciousness of what we are losing, and not look away? This is the challenge that Cavafy offered me. His poem gave me the words with which to say goodbye to my marriage, and, even as it was dissolving, the courage to feel the value it had served in my life for a period of time. I know from my own experience that a poem can be a catalyst for healing, awakening, and love. In capturing our innermost wishes and feelings, it can be the gift that we give to another and also to ourselves in a moment of parting.

I have also learned that a goodbye is an opportunity for kindness, for forgiveness, for intimacy, and ultimately for love and a deepening acceptance of life as it is instead of what it was or what we may have wanted it to be. Goodbyes can be poignant, sorrowful, sometimes a relief, and, now and then, an occasion for joy. They are always transition moments that, when embraced, can be the door to a new life both for ourselves and for others.

These ten poems help us to say goodbye in different

ways, across a spectrum of situations that we are all familiar with. The first poem, by Ellen Bass, reminds us of what I have felt today, looking out over the bay: that when we have a heightened awareness of life's fleeting impermanence, life itself becomes ever more precious and vivid. There are poems here on surviving the death of a loved one, on waving goodbye to a daughter, on looking back on a romantic love, on the loss of our younger self, and more. Then, Jane Hirshfield's poem, "When Your Life Looks Back," looks with an elegant tenderness upon the fragility and beauty of mortal life itself.

To say goodbye with all our heart is to turn a parting into a blessing. *Goodbye* is derived from the phrase "God be with you." A blessing is the offering of one heart to another; to another person, to a situation, to life itself. Isn't that what we are here for? To bless the savor of this precious moment even as it slips through our fingers? To allow its sorrow, its joy, its silence or laughter to enter our life stream and add a measure to who we are? This is the spirit of these ten poems, and the hope of this book.

1

IF YOU KNEW
by Ellen Bass

*What if you knew you'd be the last
to touch someone?
If you were taking tickets, for example,
at the theater, tearing them,
giving back the ragged stubs,
you might take care to touch that palm,
brush your fingertips
along the life line's crease.*

*When a man pulls his wheeled suitcase
too slowly through the airport, when
the car in front of me doesn't signal,
when the clerk at the pharmacy
won't say* Thank you, *I don't remember
they're going to die.*

*A friend told me she'd been with her aunt.
They'd just had lunch and the waiter,
a young gay man with plum black eyes,
joked as he served the coffee, kissed
her aunt's powdered cheek when they left.*

Then they walked half a block and her aunt
dropped dead on the sidewalk.

How close does the dragon's spume
have to come? How wide does the crack
in heaven have to split?
What would people look like
if we could see them as they are,
soaked in honey, stung and swollen,
reckless, pinned against time?

the dragon's spume

The first person I normally greet in the morning is Diego. Today, I look at him with eyes whose vision has been altered by reading this poem. Diego is from the Yucatán, but now he makes cappuccino in my local café in Sausalito. Diego is irrepressibly happy. We shake hands every day as I order my cappuccino. He invariably slides it across the counter to me with some exclamation about how beautiful the day is, whatever the weather. Even if I have just walked through a blustery wind and a smattering of rain, it seems churlish to contradict him, and I can only agree, especially when I know how far he has cycled in the small hours of the morning to get here. Yes, it is a beautiful day. Always.

Today, I take in his tiny Mayan frame; his businesslike vigor; his kind, open gaze, and I feel what this café would be like without him. It would be empty. All the locals are here because of him. Because of his warmth, his welcome, his verve. I wonder about the sad stories that hide behind his smile; the journey from his homeland, the family he has left behind, the relatives, perhaps, who never made it across the desert in Arizona. I think of him on his bicycle at four in the morning, pedaling into the wind all through

San Francisco and over the Golden Gate Bridge while the rest of us are quiet in the sleeping city.

Today, his gesture of sliding the cup over the wooden counter is lit for me with an uncommon light—the light that glows around someone as you sense that this gesture, that sentence, that smile, that look in the eyes, is already disappearing out of this moment into the timeless. Gone; gone forever. And yet a trace remains; not in the memory only, but in the feeling heart. And in the body, too; because when we see and feel like this, we are moved. For what is illuminated is the reality that, even as it disappears, the most ordinary gesture can convey the truth and beauty of a human life. I feel grateful for Diego's courage, his vulnerability to "the dragon's spume"; aware of his humanity as I am now streaming across the counter to me along with my coffee.

Aware as I am, too, of my own vulnerability, and that of everyone else in this café this morning, washed and tumbling along as we all are in the river of time, on our way to the endless ocean. Because all of us are here only for the time being; vulnerable, intrinsically vulnerable to old age, sickness, and death. Nothing will save us from this, our common fate. However puffed out our chest may be, however booming that voice of ours, however many tall buildings or stocks we own, we, too, are exquisitely, excruciatingly exposed to the fact that, sooner or later, our place will be cleared and we will be gone.

When we remember this, this poem says, something softens in us. Our judgments soften. Our hurry slows down a little, our worries return to proportion. We breathe a little easier. After all, every one of us is in the same leaky, old boat. Everyone we meet, everyone around us—the wise, the foolish, the saintly, the murderous—all of us alive today are heading together, in one great fellowship, toward the final waterfall, even as we argue, lash out at each other, care for each other, love each other, regardless of what it is we do or don't do.

This is why ours is an "exquisite" vulnerability. It is exquisite because it is so touching, so life affirming when we see through the shell of a person to the tender reality beneath. One of the women I pass in the café most mornings was in the local supermarket the other day. We had sometimes smiled in recognition, but never spoken. She always seemed busy and brisk to my eye, in charge of her day and what she was doing. When we bumped into each other in the supermarket I greeted her by saying how colorful she looked in her bright blue shirt. She said her husband had died recently, and it was the first day since then that she had felt a little alive. I am so sorry, I said. She burst into tears and clung to my shoulder, sobbing. The wave of her grief washed through and over me. I had had no idea. I would never have known. She was not in charge at all. She was just trying to do what she could to get through.

It reminded me that all of us are a hair's breadth away from death—our own or someone else's—at any moment of the day or night. All of us, whatever we may do to conceal it, are as tender inside as the down on a songbird's breast.

When a man pulls his wheeled suitcase
too slowly through the airport, when
the car in front of me doesn't signal, . . .

This is what Ellen Bass is saying in these lines: that our common vulnerability is palpable even in those who irritate us. They, too, carry the same mortal wound, and when we see this, we see their essential humanity. Then we, too, will have softened our own shell and remembered for a moment who *we* are, below the parade of our passing concerns. It is always exquisite to return to ourselves, to that quivering presence, substantial and unsayable; and know ourselves again as if for the first time.

The poems of Ellen Bass are always achingly human, just like this one, and often weave threads of grief and loss with love and starlight.

Bring me your pain, love. Spread
it out like fine rugs, silk sashes,

she says, in "Basket of Figs."[1]
In "The Moon," she sees it

framed in the windshield like a small white shell
glued to the blue silk of the afternoon.[2]

This is one of the many wonderful things about a poem: you can pour everything into it, joy and sorrow, the remarkable and the ordinary, and the poem will use all of it, turning stones into bread along the way. Just as in "If You Knew," even the man wheeling his suitcase through an airport and even the clerk in the pharmacy who won't say "Thank you" come newly alive for us when we remember that they, too, like us, are drifting toward an irrevocable finality. Bass is affirming that we are most alive when we are aware of the shadow of death that hovers over everything and perhaps especially over ourselves. It is our mortality that makes life so precious.

She brings this vividly into focus in the following stanza, which moves us from the general to the specific. She shares a graphic, startling image from her own life:

> *a young gay man with plum black eyes,*
> *joked as he served the coffee, kissed*
> *her aunt's powdered cheek when they left.*

The waiter has an air of spontaneity, and an almost feminine beauty, which is not insignificant to my mind. It suggests an ease with relatedness, with the warmth of contact, with life itself. He needs only wings to be a personification of Eros, the joyous, life-giving energy of delight and desire. And what a blessing he gives her, unknowingly—for he is the last person to touch the aunt, who walks out of the restaurant and drops down dead along the street. She was blessed with the touch of life just as she was leaving it. And he, too, was blessed without knowing it, as we are whenever we extend our hand in kindness or in generosity toward the transient, fragile life of another.

The last four lines are an accumulation of successively potent images, ending with one of the most arresting pictures of the human condition I have ever encountered:

> *What would people look like*
> *if we could see them as they are,*
> *soaked in honey, stung and swollen,*
> *reckless, pinned against time?*

Imagine looking at yourself in the mirror, or at your lover or your parents, and seeing someone "soaked in honey, stung and swollen." How forgiving your look would become, the lines in your face softening already in the glow of the truth before you. The phrase reminds me of that beautiful image of Antonio Machado's:

> *And the golden bees*
> *were making white combs*
> *and sweet honey*
> *from my old failures.*[3]

When I first heard Machado's lines, they broke open my mind to a whole new way of seeing my life. I was in amazement. Imagine the possibility that every single turn of events, however dark or disappointing the outcome, can in some circuitous way be the raw material for something that eventually surfaces with the sweetness of honey. Machado is saying that your failures can soften you, render you more permeable to worlds you may never have countenanced if you had always met with success in the world of action. The heart, like the grape, is prone to delivering its harvest in the same moment that it appears to be crushed. The beehive in your heart is humming precisely because of those failures.

Ellen Bass, too, couples our sweetness with our stung and swollen selves. Like the Japanese, who have developed an entire philosophy—wabi sabi—around the value of imperfection, she joins our beauty to our wounding. The "slings and arrows of outrageous fortune," as Hamlet puts it, can serve to unveil the inherent sweetness of our essential nature.

And our greatest wounding, the imperfection that no amount of prayer or goodness or psychotherapy will ever do anything to erase, is that we are "pinned against time." Time is both our friend and our ultimate demise. It is our friend when we awaken to the reality that this life will not always be so. When we know this from the inside, the caution that may have colored our days will dissolve like mist over the bay. With nothing to lose, knowing there can be nothing to hold on to, we can fall headlong into life at last; "reckless," like butterflies still hovering over a flower even as the collector leans forward with his net.

Far from being a tragedy, there is something poignantly

wondrous about our mortal predicament. Czeslaw Milosz, in his poem, "Encounter," captures it beautifully:

> *O my love, where are they, where are they going*
> *The flash of a hand, streak of movement, rustle of pebbles.*
> *I ask not out of sorrow, but in wonder.*[4]

I wish only that I might live out my days like this, "in wonder."

2

LOVE SONNET XCIV
by Pablo Neruda

If I die, survive me with such sheer force
that you waken the furies of the pallid and the cold,
from south to south lift your indelible eyes,
from sun to sun dream through your singing mouth.

I don't want your laughter or your steps to waver,
I don't want my heritage of joy to die.
Don't call up my person. I am absent.
Live in my absence as if in a house.

Absence is a house so vast
that inside you will pass through its walls
and hang pictures on the air.

Absence is a house so transparent
that I, lifeless, will see you, living,
and if you suffer, my love, I will die again.

if i die

There is a power, a force in this poem that runs like a river down from the first line to the last and that carries over the love of one person to another even beyond the frontiers of death. If someone is reading you this poem as lover to beloved, take in the words as a message from your lover's heart to yours, Neruda's sonnet being the bird that sings to you. Even if you are alone, you can say this poem out loud to yourself, and know that your life can continue through the life and presence of others who will survive you.

> If I die, survive me with such sheer force
> that you waken the furies of the pallid and the cold, . . .

"Survive me with such sheer force," Neruda urges his beloved, that even the dead are shaken awake. It is a tidal wave of living that he is calling for; nothing less will serve. No mere living on in memory of what was, no drifting through the days trying to pick up the pieces of a life shattered by the death of a beloved. In these first few lines I almost wonder if what Neruda wants is his revenge on Death itself. He certainly wants his love to be deathless, to continue on through the sheer vigor and vitality of the way his beloved lives her life after he has gone. There is more than a tinge of defiance here—he even says "If I die," rather than "When I die," which would be the more accurate phrase, and which reminds me of those famous lines of Dylan Thomas:

> *Do not go gentle into that good night,*
> *Old age should burn and rage at close of day;*
> *Rage, rage against the dying of the light.*[1]

Yet where Neruda departs from Thomas is in the loving melody that whispers here beneath the surface of the defiance. Neruda cares so deeply for the one he expects to leave behind that he offers this poem to her as a strong wind in her sails while she continues on her voyage through life. This is what I can hear, a siren call ringing all the way through from beginning to end: his love for her is so great, so passionate, so unstoppable that he wants to pour it into her so that she may live large enough for both of them when he is gone.

Later, looking down on her with the empty gaze of the dead, he would not have been disappointed. The lover whom Neruda addresses in this poem was the Chilean singer Matilde Urrutia. His *One Hundred Love Sonnets,* which includes this one, was published in 1960, when Neruda was in his fifties. It was dedicated to Matilde, with whom he had a clandestine relationship for the last eight years of his marriage to the Argentinian painter Delia del Carril, who was twenty years his senior.

Neruda had an international reputation as a political idealist, a diplomat, a man of letters and ideas, of big parties and global travel. He was in love with life, and he was always in love with a woman.

Throughout his life journey, he was accompanied by women. He had an affair early on with the impossibly jealous and possessive Josie Bliss. Then he married a Dutch woman, Maria Antonietta Hagenaar, in 1930, who spoke no Spanish. When they separated in 1936, he lived with his wife-to-be Delia del Carril. They separated in 1955, and Neruda spent the rest of his life with Matilde.

Matilde Urrutia was the inspiration for much of Neruda's later poetry. While he was still married to Delia, Neruda would send Matilde love poems daily. During this early part of their love affair, the great Mexican artist Diego Rivera painted Matilde's portrait with a profile of Neruda concealed in her thick dark hair. It was the lovers' secret. After their marriage, in 1966, Matilde remained his beloved companion until his death, in 1973.

Neruda was in the hospital in Chile when Augusto Pinochet seized power from the democratically elected Salvadore Allende. He was so stricken by what was happening in his country that he suffered a heart attack and died within days of Pinochet taking control. But Matilde amply fulfilled his call for her to live large until she herself died in 1985. She became the persecuted widow of a national hero when Pinochet tried to erase the collective memory of Neruda, who had been a committed communist. A fervent human rights activist for the rest of her life, she repeatedly courted danger by attending rallies and demonstrations. Her book, *My Life with Pablo Neruda,* was published posthumously.

Death, after all, is always the shadow of love, however young or old we are, for everything, even that which we would wish to last forever, has its season, and no more. Or is it really so? Neruda's beautiful sonnet, in which love and death are entwined from beginning to end, takes up the time-honored romantic theme—that love can survive all. Love will always outlive death. Love is the air of the soul, I would say, and the soul does not die because there is no end to love.

For Neruda, love will survive through the living; through the "indelible eyes" of his lover, and in her "singing mouth." It will survive in her laughter and in her unwavering step. In another sonnet from the same collection, number LIX, he says

> *I want your ears still to hear the wind, I want you*
> *to sniff the sea's aroma that we loved together,*
> *to continue to walk on the sand we walk on.*[2]

In sonnet XCIV, he says

> *I don't want my heritage of joy to die.*

Our "heritage of joy": this, Neruda says, is what we have to give to the world and to those who live on. Not our money, our property, nor even our good name, so much as the legacy of joy that we have accrued over a lifetime. Pablo Neruda was a man who lived large, a man with the greatest appetite for life; and over his lifetime he drank life's brew of joy and sorrow down to the dregs. This is what he wants to live on; not through his memory, nor even through his poetry, but through the "sheer force" of the woman he loves and whom he expects to survive him.

Then the sonnet takes an unexpected turn.

> *Don't call up my person. I am absent.*
> *Live in my absence as if in a house.*

For Neruda, committed communist that he was, nothing survives death unless it continues on somehow in the living. No use, then, in summoning his presence after he has gone. He will be unreachable, and will never return. No use singing his praises or lamenting the loss of him. Better to have the courage to fully accept and live in the truth of his absence.

Some trace of the wondrous hovers in these lines. Imagine living in absence as in a vast mansion, an absence so complete that you can walk through walls and hang "pictures on the air." Nothing and nowhere to hold on to. How vast the world would seem; how utterly free you would feel. Free of the past, free of the future, free to swim in the present, weightless.

And then in the last stanza, Neruda gives a final twist to the sonnet:

> *Absence is a house so transparent*
> *that I, lifeless, will see you, living, . . .*

So he does continue to exist after all. Though he will be lifeless, he will still see his beloved, who lives on in his absence. Not only will he see her, but he will die all over again if he sees her suffer. He needs her to go on with her life in the full embrace of his absence. Anything less would be unbearable for him, and Matilde Urrutia does not disappoint. Perhaps her full embrace of her own life after Neruda's death is what a true goodbye really is: the deepest letting go.

3

HOW IT WILL HAPPEN, WHEN
by Dorianne Laux

There you are, exhausted from another night of crying,
curled up on the couch, the floor, at the foot of the bed,

anywhere you fall you fall down crying, half amazed
at what the body is capable of, not believing you can cry

anymore. And there they are: his socks, his shirt, your
underwear, and your winter gloves, all in a loose pile

next to the bathroom door, and you fall down again.
Someday, years from now, things will be different:

the house clean for once, everything in its place, windows
shining, sun coming in easily now, skimming across

the thin glaze of wax on the wood floor. You'll be peeling
an orange or watching a bird leap from the edge of the
*   rooftop*

next door, noticing how, for an instant, her body is trapped
in the air, only a moment before gathering the will to fly

into the ruff at her wings, and then doing it: flying.
You'll be reading, and for a moment you'll see a word

you don't recognize, a simple word like cup or gate or
    wisp
and you'll ponder over it like a child discovering
    language.

Cup, you'll say it over and over until it begins to make
    sense,
and that's when you'll say it, for the first time, out loud:
    He's dead.

He's not coming back, and it will be the first time you
    believe it.

you'll be peeling an orange

This poem sweeps me up, whirls me around, and sets me down again a different person. I could never have imagined a grief as fierce, as ferocious as this. I myself have never experienced such a visceral outpouring. I can only bow to the immensity of grief that lies stored in the human soul.

I was in bed, more than a decade ago now, the sun streaming already through the window, when my partner came in the room to tell me my father had died. He was walking up the stairs, my mother behind him, when he stopped, and leaned over slightly. "I think this is it," he said. And it was. My mother helped him up to their bed, and he lay down and died. He was eighty-six. He had never had a day's illness in his life.

As I lay there absorbing the news, I felt my whole being expand into a vibrant silence. Unthinkingly, I spread my arms out wide. It had happened, as it was bound to do. And with a grace and ease that I could only wish everyone would know.

My mother died several years later, at the age of eighty-two. Following a stroke, she had to leave her apartment and spend her last year in a nursing home. A determinedly self-sufficient woman, she had to suffer the humbling necessity of being washed and fed. When she eventually died, my siblings and I were thankful that she had been spared further indignity. At her funeral tears flowed, but quietly, and with waves of gratitude for the loving presence she had been for us.

She and my father are never coming back—I knew that from the moment they died—but their presence envelops me now as it always did, and I often catch myself talking to one or the other of them as I walk through my garden gate or sit alone in the growing shadows of evening. Unlike Neruda, for me their absence offers no contradiction to their continuing presence; not a presence I think back on, but that I am aware of now, in my current flurry of days.

But what another kind of desolation it must be, to experience the loss of a beloved partner, husband, or wife. It is in the natural course of events to expect one's parents to die in one's lifetime, but someone you share your life with is part of you. Your identity is entwined with theirs; you were a unit, and there is no filling the gaping chasm that one of you leaves when you die. I can feel that, imagine it, but I do not know it. Only one of my close friends has died, and no one I have ever lived with. Perhaps it is because I am a stranger to the grief in this poem that it felt like an initiation of sorts when I first read it, a baptism into a dimension of being human that I never knew. A poem can do this for us.

But Dorianne Laux knows grief with every cell of her being. She must, for these lines to pour from her pen; a remarkable intensity, sustained all the way to the quiet of the other shore at the end. Laux is one of America's finest poets of personal witness. She uses the grist of her own life to touch universal themes that can strike to the heart of even a reader like me, who has had no direct experience of what she is describing. In doing so, she binds me in that much more closely with our shared human story. This poem is in her volume *Smoke,* and it is one of a few in that collection that address the death of her lover from cancer.

"[C]urled up on the couch, the floor, the foot of the bed"—the alliteration of that hard *k* somehow captures the spasm, the angularity of the body racked with grief. And there is that part of consciousness that is able to witness it all, "half amazed at what the body is capable of," amazed, too, that there are still tears left to shed. It's true that in moments of extreme intensity, as in an imminent car crash, the witness part of us watches from some other, stiller place. I am reminded of the ancient image, common both in the East and in the West, of two birds at a fountain, the one drinking while the other looks on.

The next sentence in this prose poem beautifully captures the intermingling of two human hearts who have lived and loved each other through the years; and it does so not by naming shared joys ("Death is not romantic," she says in her poem "Abscheid's Symphony") but by describing a jumble of clothes, his and hers:

> *And there they are: his socks, his shirt, your*
> *underwear, and your winter gloves, all in a loose pile*
>
> *next to the bathroom door, and you fall down again.*

In this one sentence she gives life and meaning to the most forgettable details of a life lived with another. She brings it so graphically before our eyes that the image lingers in my mind, trailing the smell and feel of intimacy, long after my eyes have traveled on down the page. When an image literally touches you like this, you know it is doing its work, which is to evoke a physical sensation in one or more of our senses.

This heightened awareness of detail, she says, again in "Abscheid's Symphony," is precisely what she would love to be free of:

> *For months now all I've wanted is the blessing*
> *of inattention, to move carefully from room to room*
> *in my small house, numb with forgetfulness.*[1]

But fortunately for us, she is not numb. She is in the heightened state that can accompany the vicinity of death, and so everything is brought to life for us, the reader— even a pile of clothes by the bathroom door.

Even without the acute awareness of life that can accompany the presence of death, Laux is always a poet who finds profound value, even transcendent value, in the everyday. The luminous, the exalted, if it exists at all, does so right here, in the humdrum acts and paraphernalia of ordinary living.

In *The Poet's Companion*, the guide to writing she cowrote with Kim Addonizio, the very first chapter begins with these words:

> We've been told again and again to write about what we know, but we don't trust that advice. We think our lives are dull, ordinary, boring. Other people have lives worthy of poetry, but not us. And what are the "great" poems about? The big subjects: death, desire, the nature of existence. They ask the big questions. Who are we? Why are we here? Where are we going? We find it difficult to believe those subjects, those questions, can be explored and contained in a poem about working at a fast food restaurant, a poem about our best friend, a poem about washing the dishes, tarring the roof or taking a bus across town. . . .
>
> The trick is to find out what we know, challenge what we know, own what we know, and then give it away in language. I love my brother, I hate winter, I always lose my keys. . . . Good writing works from a simple premise: your experience is not yours alone, but in some sense is a metaphor for everyone's.[2]

In this poem she is giving away in language what she knows about death. And what she knows, it goes on to say, is that there will come a time, later, perhaps much later, when it will all be different. The world will have tilted back to normal. You will have tilted back to normal. Your house will be clean, everything will be in its place, the "sun coming in easily now."

The light will have returned, the shadows will have fallen into yesterday. But though the light may come "in easily now," it is not some ephemeral, insubstantial element that takes Laux's thinking heavenward, or toward some wistful, nostalgic reflection. No, the light actually gains weight and materiality by "skimming across / the thin glaze of wax on the wood floor." Amazing image! Again, she evokes a physical sensation. I can actually feel that light making its way across her shiny floor. It has become a tangible part of the physical world she lives in.

There will come a time, she says, when everything will have become ordinary again. "You'll be peeling / an orange . . . You'll be reading." Someone I know who lost a beloved partner in the prime of life said she would sometimes feel guilty in the midst of a mundane chore— opening the curtains, perhaps, or when talking to a friend—because she was still here and he was . . . where was he now? But there is no guilt in this poem, no sense of something unfinished or incomplete. On the contrary, Dorianne Laux is fully here, in her house, more fully aware than many of us are of every concrete detail in the living moment. (Which is why she can write a poem like this.)

Then she reaches this extraordinary moment that is carried along on the image of reading a book, reading a book and coming upon a word that you do not understand: "a simple word like cup or gate or wisp." Have you ever had that peculiar, unsettling experience? I know I have. Dori-anne Laux must have, too. Time stops and the utterly familiar becomes utterly strange; completely other to your known experience. In that moment there is a rare form of seeing, a rare form of wakefulness. It is as if you are seeing something for the very first time, something you may have known forever, but that now assumes an actuality, a concrete here-ness, that it had never assumed before.

This is why seeing a word as if for the first time is such a precise image for her purposes. Because it is then that she can say for the first time out loud the words that she could never have embraced and fully understood before: "He's dead." The full awareness of that fact has finally sunk in to the degree that she can say the words, making it a fact to accompany all the other facts of that moment—the light on the floor, the peeling of an orange, reading. The reality has become as concrete and also as ordinary as every other fact—"He's not coming back."

There is something graceful, even luminous, about these final lines. They are clean of regret; they convey the clear edges, the finality of the reality of her lover's death, in a way that is utterly unsentimental. Their grace, I believe, is in the profound acceptance they convey; a stone has dropped to the bottom of her pond. The irreversible truth has finally sunk in, and with it, I imagine, a quiet, a rest has come upon her soul. And yet this resolution only occurs at the end of a poem that begins with one of the most heartrending depictions of grief I have ever read.

Dorianne Laux becomes her grief in this poem. She inhabits it with every limb and cell of her being. She breathes it in, drinks it down, shakes and shudders with it; lies exhausted with it. She seems to know somehow, with Kahlil Gibran, that

> *Your pain is the breaking of the shell that encloses your understanding.*[3]

The understanding that comes at this poem's end is a result of her feeling and bearing the pain that came at the beginning. To come to the surface again and see with new eyes, Laux is suggesting here, you must first dive down, deep down, without even knowing if you will ever surface again. This, it seems to me, is the essence of this poem. It reminds me of what David Whyte points to in his poem "The Well of Grief":

> *Those who will not slip beneath*
> *the still surface of the well of grief . . .*
> *will never know the source from which we drink, . . .*[4]

Laux has been there, down below the surface of the well of grief, and the wisdom she gathered along the way has formed into the gift of this poem.

4

THE LOST HOTELS OF PARIS
by Jack Gilbert

The Lord gives everything and charges
by taking it back. What a bargain.
Like being young for a while. We are
allowed to visit hearts of women,
to go into their bodies so we feel
no longer alone. We are permitted
romantic love with its bounty and half-life
of two years. It is right to mourn
for the small hotels of Paris that used to be
when we used to be. My mansard looking
down on Notre Dame every morning is gone,
and me listening to the bell at night.
Venice is no more. The best Greek islands
have drowned in acceleration. But it's the having
not the keeping that is the treasure.
Ginsberg came to my house one afternoon
and said he was giving up poetry
because it told lies, that language distorts.

I agreed, but asked what we have
that gets it right even that much.
We look up at the stars and they are
not there. We see the memory
of when they were, once upon a time.
And that too is more than enough.

more than enough

"I don't want to be at peace," Jack Gilbert said, on turning eighty years old. "I think of heaven and think that I wouldn't want to just float around in happiness in a place without imperfection, where you don't fall in love. I picture everything there being one color. I can't imagine anything better than being here on earth." *Refusing Heaven,* which won the National Book Critics Circle Award in 2005, includes this marvelous poem, "The Lost Hotels of Paris."

In 2009, at the age of eighty-four and conspicuously frail, Gilbert surprised everyone by coming out with another volume, *The Dance Most of All.* With most poetry collections, I usually light upon no more than a couple of poems that strike me to the core. In *Refusing Heaven,* and also in *The Dance Most of All,* shards of light rise up to greet me on every other page.

Gilbert is a profound lover of life, and he is not about to roll over sooner than he has to. He is a "serious romantic," to use his own term, never satisfied with easy answers. He relishes as always the deep questions, those awoken by love, loss, and death. His small body of work—*Refusing*

Heaven was just his fourth publication in eighty years—
is an unflinching exploration of the map of the human
heart. His poetry represents a lifelong spiritual quest for
authenticity, and his voice is that of the outsider; of one
who consciously avoided tenure and the comforts of suc-
cess for the rigors of poetry as a means of transcendence.

Gilbert was already beginning to suffer from dementia
when he wrote the poems in *Refusing Heaven*. The open-
ing lines of "The Lost Hotels of Paris," then, are no mere
philosophizing.

> *The Lord gives everything and then charges*
> *by taking it back. What a bargain!*

This is Gilbert's present reality. The Lord gave him
everything: a piercing insight, a rigorous attention to the
truth of his experience and the words needed to convey
it, an acute sensibility that was able to register and convey
the subtlest layers of human feeling. And all of it now is
beginning to fall away. Yet he continues to persist in writ-
ing poetry like this. Poetry that manages to combine a lyri-
cal mix of anguish and grace; joyous, celebratory poetry
even when the subject is loss and the passing of time.

Even so, these first two lines refer to his illness merely by
implication. They point less to his physical condition than
to a lifelong way of seeing the world. In a 2006 NPR inter-
view with Debbie Elliott he said, "Sure it's tough, we're all
going to die, there's a lot of injustice in the world, but what
a bargain. If you balance it out, what a balance. There's a

lot of things I don't like. I don't like the fact that my hair is thinning. I don't like the fact that two of the women I loved died. But given that, what a wonderful privilege to be allowed to breathe, to see, to feel, to smell, to love. It's baffling, the sweetness of what we're allowed."

That's Jack Gilbert's spirit in a single paragraph. Now, his strength and his faculties fading,

> *I crank my heart even so and it turns over*

he says in another of his poems, "A Kind of Courage."[1]

Jack Gilbert was an outsider from the very beginning. He was born in Pittsburgh in 1925, and his father worked in the circus for a time and died after falling out of the window of a Prohibition men's club when Jack was ten years old. Jack dropped out of school early and took various odd jobs, including a spell as a Fuller Brush salesman, until he was admitted to the University of Pittsburgh through a clerical error. It was at the university that he began writing poetry, and after graduation he moved to postwar Paris and spent several years wandering around in Europe. He returned to the States in 1956 and lived for several years in the creative ferment of the Bay Area, becoming a central figure in the literary and poetry scene there.

In 1962, at the age of thirty-seven, he won the Yale Younger Poets prize for his first volume of poetry, which was also nominated for a Pulitzer. Suddenly he was a literary phenomenon, and his unusually good looks—which have lasted into his eighties—landed him not only on the cover of *Esquire* but also in *Vogue* and in *Teen* magazine. Yet Gilbert didn't cash in with a quick follow-up volume. He left the temptation of literary fame and fortune in America to roam around Europe again, this time on a Guggenheim Fellowship. He chose a deliberate and radical cultivation of solitude over the easy allure of celebrity, and was away for twenty years or more, accompanied by a succession of three women—muses all, the love and loss of whom pervade all his work.

For most of his life he has lived in the margins, eking out a simple existence on Santorini, a Greek island in the Aegean; on a houseboat in Kashmir, in Japan, in France, and in the backcountry of western Massachussets. He has never owned a home and has only driven a car twice in his life. Gilbert's long and adventurous journey is testimony to a life of principle.

In "The Lost Hotels of Paris," he offers a beautiful elegy to those places and people he has loved in his life who are no longer here, including a succession of his own younger selves. Not surprisingly, since his life has been so entwined with them, he begins with women and their place in his life.

> *We are*
> *allowed to visit hearts of women,*
> *to go into their bodies so we feel*
> *no longer alone. . . .*

Some critics have taken a feminist stance to Gilbert's response to women and have criticized him for treating them as objects of desire and muses rather than as real people with lives and destinies of their own. I don't agree. His life and work are suffused with an awe and profound respect for the women he has known and loved. A woman for Gilbert is essentially unknowable, and communion with her serves as a gateway for both into the numinous, the transcendent realm beyond the separate ego and beyond desire itself. In another poem, he asks

> *What is the word for*
> *that still thing I have hunted inside them*
> *for so long?*[2]

Gilbert often uses the phrase "we are allowed," signifying permission granted by some power beyond our personal will. It is a condition of grace, then, that allows a man "to visit" a woman's heart. "To visit" but not to stay: everything given is taken back. Nothing lasts. It's the Buddhist teaching on impermanence in poetic form. And then, to enter her body is a respite from loneliness for both of them, for

> *Loneliness is the mother's milk of America,*[3]

he says in the poem "Meanwhile." The poet Linda Gregg was his wife and companion during his travels in the sixties through Greece and Europe. Later, he was married for eleven years to the Japanese woman Michiko Nogami, until she died of cancer in the early eighties at the age of thirty-six. In "The Mistake," Gilbert writes

> *It is worth having the heart broken*
> *a blessing to hurt for eighteen years*
> *because a woman is dead. . . .*[4]

In the same way, "we are permitted romantic love"; and for Gilbert it is worth it even though it has a half-life of only two years. How easy it is to be cynical about the foolishness of romance; to bemoan its fleeting, illusory nature, and all the pain and suffering it can cause. But for Gilbert, who is the opposite of a cynic, romantic love is a bargain. Every experience on this earth is a bargain; and all the more precious for its passing.

Romantic love was a bargain for me a few years ago, when I fell in love with an unavailable woman, for, well, about two years. I was not twenty; I was sixty, which made it seem all the more foolish. We are never allowed a preview of the eventual outcome of such an encounter. All we can know is that we will not be who we once were, and our life will not be what it once was. Love is always a gift, and though its form may change and even fade away, the essence of it—the love that has burst open our heart and ushered in a deeper, more vital way of living—can never be taken away. Being cooked in the fire of love, being stewed in our own juices you might say, contributes to the making of who we are. We are all of us so achingly human, and if the cynic is kept at bay, we emerge from love's fire more tender and more open, however brief our loving may have been.

Gilbert's poem proceeds to the passing of places that he knew at earlier times in his life.

> *It is right to mourn*
> *for the small hotels of Paris that used to be*
> *when we used to be. My mansard looking*
> *down on Notre Dame every morning is gone,*
> *and me listening to the bell at night.*

My own small hotel in Paris, now long gone, was just along from Gilbert's, on the Île Saint-Louis. It had a blue door with a large brass knocker and a small brass plate that said Hôtel de L'Île. My room was up a narrow, winding staircase on the fifth floor, and the window looked out onto the brown waters of the Seine. The person that I was then stayed in that room with his love, whenever they crossed the Channel from London. He wore a French beret and a three-quarter-length leather jacket. She wore a blue scarf wrapped around her head like an Arab and white silk pants that would shimmer in the wind gusting in from the river. Like the Jack Gilbert who listened to the bell at night, those two lovebirds have gone the way of all things. And "it is right to mourn" them.

For the mourning is not a wish for them to return, but an elegy to their having been in the first place.

Along with Paris, the rest of the world has changed, as it must. Nothing is as it was when we were younger.

> *Venice is no more. The best Greek islands*
> *have drowned in acceleration.*

Gilbert is rarely, if ever, sentimental. These lines are not some wistful longing for a more idyllic past. They are a statement of fact. The Venice of even twenty years ago, not to mention forty years, is no more. In the sixties and early seventies, most Greek islands were still far-flung outposts of a traditional culture that had barely changed in centuries. I remember arriving just before dawn in the crescent bay of Santorini, the island where Gilbert lived for a time, in the summer of 1965, somewhat queasy from the journey from Crete in an old boat that had groaned its way all through the night, overloaded with goats and people and chickens. I remember, too, the cries of the boatmen as they rowed out in the dark to pick us up in handfuls and take us to shore, where braying donkeys were waiting to jog us up the steep cliffs to the tiny village above.

Those days are gone now. Santorini was a remote place then, barely known to the outside world. No more than half a dozen foreigners were there when the Housden of that time stumbled ashore in August of 1965. One of them was probably Jack Gilbert. Today Santorini is featured on all the Greek tourist posters and is the favorite destination of cruise ships. Like all the islands, it has "drowned in acceleration."

> *But it's the having*
> *not the keeping that is the treasure.*

Santorini as Gilbert knew it entered not only his eyes but his sinews, his very cells, like anything we have loved. It is alive in him still, not just in memory but in his being, as it is alive in mine. This is why there is no need for nostalgia, for some hopeless clinging to a romanticized past.

Poetry can capture the essence of an experience. It can bless the past even as it mourns it, and this is what Gilbert is doing in this poem. This is why he disagrees with Ginsberg, who said

> *he was giving up poetry*
> *because it told lies, that language distorts.*

Ginsberg would often visit Gilbert in the early sixties, when he lived up a dirt track in an old cabin in Sausalito, over the Golden Gate Bridge, which is where I happen to live now. Their friendship was combative, and Gilbert didn't think much of Ginsberg's work until the day he walked in with a sheaf of papers, the beginning of a new poem. Gilbert was impressed. It was the beginning of "Howl."

Gilbert agreed that language distorts,

> *but asked what we have*
> *that gets it right even that much.*

We do what we can, we use what we have. Jack Gilbert has never given up; not on poetry, nor on love, nor on life. We never see the stars as they are, he says in the last lines of this poem, only the memory of them the way they once were.

And that too is more than enough.

5

WAVING GOOD-BYE
by Gerald Stern

*I wanted to know what it was like before we
had voices and before we had bare fingers and before we
had minds to move us through our actions
and tears to help us over our feelings,
so I drove my daughter through the snow to meet her
   friend
and filled her car with suitcases and hugged her
as an animal would, pressing my forehead against her,
walking in circles, moaning, touching her cheek,
and turned my head after them as an animal would,
watching helplessly as they drove over the ruts,
her smiling face and her small hand just visible
over the giant pillows and coat hangers
as they made their turn into the empty highway.*

watching my daughter
drive away

Gerald Stern can be too excessive for some readers, too exuberant in his cascade of emotions for the handheld info-world we live in. Our culture has cultivated cool. It has elevated irony and cleverness, along with their shadows of relativism and nihilism, to the height of contemporary style. Never mind. For me and many others, Gerald Stern rocks. I love how he gives free rein to feeling. I love how he weeps and trembles across the pages of his poetry, how he extols the value of tenderness and defends beauty at every turn, even as it is drowning beneath a tide of ugliness.

A Walt Whitman for our time, it is often said. And what could be wrong with that? Surely we need large and full-blooded spirits to shudder across our stage and remind us what this living is for. In the place of Whitman's bugle calls and grand democratic urges, Gerald Stern returns us to the intimate world of the interior life and also to the living, breathing world of wild things and the animal kingdom. Animals run freely through all his volumes of poetry. They even, as in "The Dog," speak to us from the grave. They lie dead by the side of the road, too, as in his most anthologized poem, "Behaving Like a Jew," or like the squirrel in "I Remember Galileo," they recall for Stern the peculiar mind of man.

·   Gerald Stern was born in the same year as Jack Gilbert, 1925, and in the same town, Pittsburgh. They both went to the University of Pittsburgh.

> *I think of Gilbert all the time now, what*
> *we said on our long walks in Pittsburgh, how*
> *lucky we were to live in New York, how strange*
> *his great fame and my obscurity. . . .*[1]

Stern would have to wait fifteen more years after the success of Gilbert's first collection for his own eruption into the limelight with *Lucky Life,* which was published in 1977, when Stern was forty-eight. But whereas Gilbert turned his back on fame and chose to live a life of solitude and relative poverty in Europe for the next twenty years, Stern, except for a year of postgraduate studies in Paris in 1949, moved around the States from university to university, including a fifteen-year stint as senior poet at the Iowa Writers' Workshop. He has published fifteen volumes of poetry as well as a series of essays. It was Stern who became the famous one, it turns out, while Gilbert remained content with years of obscurity after his initial success.

"Waving Good-bye" is classic Stern. You can find it in *This Time: New and Selected Poems,* which was published in 1998 and won the National Book Award. I acknowledge that I am a stranger to the emotions Stern unrolls for us here. I have one son, but never have I said goodbye to him with the animal ferocity that Stern unleashes in this poem. Perhaps it would be different if I had a daughter, like Stern; but I doubt it, for I was raised Anglican in the genteel air of Bath in England. Stern is of Eastern European Jewish stock, and a certain biblical intensity pervades all his work—not to mention a profound Judaic sense of time and loss. Doubtless this explains in part the attraction of his work for me. He paints in colors that have rarely crossed my palette, and leads me to see unknown coves and corners of my own humanity there.

> *I wanted to know what it was like before we*
> *had voices and before we had bare fingers and before we*
> *had minds to move us through our actions*
> *and tears to help us over our feelings, . . .*

I have never thought to wonder what this would be like. Stern reaches down deep in his psyche for some antediluvian stratum in which we are barely distinguishable from our ancestors the apes; to a layer of our humanity where the separate ego is still a developmental stage in the future. Before our fingers were bare, they were covered in hair. Before we had language, we were grunting, nudging, shouldering creatures. And like apes today, we didn't cry then.

Stern wants to go down there so that he can hug his daughter

as an animal would, pressing my forehead against her,
walking in circles, moaning, touching her cheek,
and turned my head after them as an animal would,
watching helplessly as they drove over the ruts, . . .

They surge along on a great tide of life, these glorious lines; a tide that swells and washes over the mind of this reader, and swirls him down somewhere below his usual cerebral knowing of this incredible world. Stern's "moaning" becomes music in these lines, the wailing music of the shtetl where his grandmother lived; the music he and his parents danced to in their living room in 1945,

the three of us whirling and singing, the three of us
screaming and falling, as if we were dying,
as if we could never stop— . . .[2]

Gerald Stern has ready access to these nether regions. But then he was nurtured in an environment friendly to and familiar with the mammalian sense of touch and nuzzle, of a close community of praise and mourning. How many of us have danced around the family living room with our parents? Not to mention "whirling and singing . . . screaming and falling." The territory he sings into being in "Waving Good-bye" is hardly foreign to him.

For me it is novel, and yet not strange. Stern draws me in on the lilt of his lines. I can feel the hug he gives his daughter, his forehead pressed against hers. I can see and also feel him

walking in circles, moaning, touching her cheek,

and some urge from a world usually obscure to me makes me want to join him there, my shoulders hunched and pushing myself forward in some ceremonial rhythm round and round as in some long-forgotten ritual of the native world.

For this is a rite of passage Stern unfolds before us in this poem. The end of an era, of a way of life, of a particular kind of relationship—all this is taking place here in the hugging and moaning and walking in circles. All of this, not just the daughter, is what Gerald Stern is waving goodbye to. We can assume that Stern's daughter is leaving home, probably for the first time. Going to college, perhaps, or to the big city. Stern's role as father is changing as a result, along with her role as daughter.

She is becoming an adult, striking out on her own, responsible now in a greater degree for herself. The era of the child is over. But it is not only she but her father who has to say goodbye to a time they have known that has passed. This is why, I think, there is such powerful emotion in this poem, and such deep authenticity. A rite of passage lifts everyone who takes part in it beyond the merely personal realm. In a rite of passage one is reenacting a time-honored and universal moment, joining hands with all the generations who have passed through that same hoop before. The daughter or son leaving home is one such moment. Stern feels this viscerally. This is why the feeling tone is so robust, and why there is no trace of nostalgia or sentimentality in his poem.

Sentimentality, after all, occurs when the mind attempts to draw upon the energies of the heart to express *an idea* it has of a feeling. Sentimentality is, finally, cerebral. It starts with an idea and tries to whip up the emotion to fuel the idea. This is why sentimentality is never authentic. In "Waving Good-bye," Stern does the opposite. He draws the mind down into the heart; and lower still, down into the belly, and gives himself over—gives his cerebral self over—to the trembling and tenderness and vulnerability of the reality of loss.

For there is a profound sense of loss in this poem, and at the same time a primal, almost ecstatic joy. As at the Wailing Wall, in Jerusalem, where the Jews lament the loss of their temple and yet celebrate the continuing presence there of God. Stern's loss is expressed most dramatically in these lines:

> *and turned my head after them as an animal would,*
> *watching helplessly as they drove over the ruts, . . .*

Who hasn't felt at some time in their life the soft and longing gaze of a dog or a horse as they turn their head to watch you leave? Rumi says,

> *Listen to the moan of a dog for its master.*
> *That whining is the connection.*[3]

Stern watches "helplessly" as his daughter leaves and turns into the "empty highway." He is helpless before the movement of time. There is nothing he can do to make things the way they once were; and yet he willingly stands there, heart and soul wide open, utterly given not only to the reality of what he is losing but also to the new and empty space that is opening up in life for them both. "Empty" is desolate, and in her leaving a great emptiness lies before him. But "empty" is also new ground, clear of the past. In emptying himself out, Stern allows himself to be open to the new, to whatever may be next. Because if there is one thing in life we can be sure of, it is that there will always be a next. Until there isn't.

6

THOSE WINTER SUNDAYS
by Robert Hayden

Sundays too my father got up early
and put his clothes on in the blueblack cold,
then with cracked hands that ached
from labor in the weekday weather made
banked fires blaze. No one ever thanked him.

I'd wake and hear the cold splintering, breaking.
When the rooms were warm, he'd call,
and slowly I would rise and dress,
fearing the chronic angers of that house.

Speaking indifferently to him,
who had driven out the cold
and polished my good shoes as well.
What did I know, what did I know
of love's austere and lonely offices?

what did i know?

I would like to think that this poem is Robert Hayden's way of saying the goodbye that he never managed to say before his father died. It is never too late, even if decades have passed, to feel what was not felt and to say what was not said—even if the person is no longer there to hear you and your farewell must live on in a poem. For a true farewell is a fulfillment more than an ending, a bond of love that joins you to someone even as they are leaving. A farewell such as the one in this poem will sing on, like the head of Orpheus floating and praising, down the river of all our days.

Robert Hayden was born in a poor ghetto neighborhood of Detroit known as Paradise Valley. It was 1913. When he was eighteen months old, he was given to the family next door because his parents had separated before he was born and his mother could not afford to keep him. The child had no birth certificate, and his foster parents renamed him with their family name.

His new father was a manual laborer, but even so

Sundays too my father got up early

Sundays would normally have been a day of rest, the one day in the week when a laborer would not have to get up early. So the little word "too" carries more than its usual weight in this first line. Even on his one day of rest, his father would get up before anyone else to warm the house for his family. He would "put his clothes on in the blueblack cold." In an earlier version of the poem, Hayden wrote "stiffening cold." What a difference a word can make! "Blueblack cold": you can see it, the ice on the doorstep of this Michigan house deep in winter, the back of his father's hand "blueblack" in the freezing cold. You can hear it too, its cracking with the alliterative *k* of "black" and "cold," picked up in the next line with "cracked" and "ached." I remember how the skin on blue hands flakes and chaps in English winters and little red crevices, sore and stinging, split open the fold of the knuckles. Hayden's father would have lived with that through every Michigan winter, far colder than any in England.

I think of my own father, who rose all his life before dawn to start his day as a delivery driver for Unilever, his employer for forty years. Some winter mornings in the old stone cottage outside of Bath I would wake briefly as the front door closed and see the sheen of frost on my faded red eiderdown. He would come home in the evening just as I was going to bed, and in my teens I would feel the indifference fostered by our lack of shared warmth and attention. I did not appreciate then, obvious as it may seem now, that his years of unstinting labor were all that kept us fed and warm. I would only remember how my mother, the day before payday, would have nothing left in her purse until he returned with the next week's wages.

Hayden's foster father had the instinctual kindness that was probably a stoic mixture of duty and love. Always the first one to rise, he would light the fires in the house day after day, week after week, without ever expecting or receiving thanks from the rest of his family, whom he would wake only when the rooms were warmed. The "chronic angers" that the young Hayden would fear as he went downstairs were the grim contribution of, not his father, but his foster mother, who was deeply unhappy in her marriage. It is only much later in life, in this poem, that Robert Hayden recognizes the silent ways his father cared for him and his family.

> *Speaking indifferently to him,*
> *who had driven out the cold*
> *and polished my good shoes as well.*

These lines remind me of some others in an unpublished poem that my friend Sherry Anderson wrote for her father:

> *you gave me everything I needed*
> *though I didn't know it then*
> *though I wanted so much more*
> *and differently*

And now not remembering even
how I began this poem
let alone when you were angry and
scared me

All just words now and this
is turning out to be
a love letter
to you gone all these years . . .[1]

And so it was for me, who only later in life came to feel the love for my father that my teenage blindness had denied me earlier. Hayden's foster father was a devout Baptist, and his family would go every Sunday morning to church. This is why he would be sure to polish his adopted son's "good shoes."

He also encouraged his adopted son in his education. The boy suffered from poor sight and, unable to participate in sports, spent his time reading. He won a scholarship to Detroit City College and went on to study with W. H. Auden at the University of Michigan. Auden was an influential guide in the development of his writing, and Hayden's first book of poems, *Heart-Shape in the Dust,* appeared in 1940. Hayden achieved international recognition in 1966 when he won the grand prize for poetry at the First World Festival of Negro Arts in Dakar, Senegal. In 1976 he became the first African American to take the position of poet laureate. He had traveled a very long and often lonely road from the poverty-stricken black ghetto of Detroit.

"What did I know": to have this phrase twice at the end of the poem is to cry out in regret at his own ignorance and immaturity—not in self-recrimination, it seems to me, but in wonder at the way youth (and not only youth, but enduring resentment) can obscure the love it has been receiving all along.

The last line of the poem is one of those that can burn itself into the memory for years: "love's austere and lonely offices." His father performed love's offices every day. They were lonely, not affectionate offerings. He loved in the only way he knew how, which was through action and silent service, like so many men. And he received no thanks, no recognition for his labors or evident return of love. But "offices" are surely like that: acts of service undertaken without thought of reward. The word has a religious connotation, suggesting a dedication or submission to a purpose higher than one's own self-interest.

This poem is itself a kind of office. It is a transparent song of love. It not only soars to wherever his father is now but also includes and redeems through love the narrower and younger Robert Hayden himself. It serves as testimony to the beautiful lines at the end of the poem "An Arundel Tomb," by Philip Larkin:

> *Our almost-instinct almost true:*
> *What will survive of us is love.*[2]

7

it may not always be so; and i say
by e. e. cummings

it may not always be so; and i say
that if your lips, which i have loved, should touch
another's, and your dear strong fingers clutch
his heart, as mine in time not far away;
if on another's face your sweet hair lay
in such a silence as i know, or such
great writhing words as, uttering overmuch,
stand helplessly before the spirit at bay;

if this should be, i say if this should be-
you of my heart, send me a little word;
that i may go unto him, and take his hands,
saying, Accept all happiness from me.
Then shall i turn my face, and hear one bird
sing terribly afar in the lost lands.

heart to heart

This poem is one of the most profoundly moving testimonies I have ever read on love, and letting go even as you love. It appeared in Cummings's first collection of poetry, *Tulips and Chimneys,* in 1923. After World War I Cummings was a leading figure in the movement to demolish Victorian proprieties and experiment with all kinds of liberation, sexual and social as well as literary, so it is not certain which woman in his life he may have had in mind in this poem.

We do know that in 1918 he fell in love with Elaine Orr, the wife of his mentor, Scofield Thayer, editor of *The Dial,* the Modernist literary magazine that first published Cummings's work. Cummings and Orr had a daughter, Nancy, in 1919, while Orr was still married to Thayer. These years were doubtless full of uncertainty for all concerned, and this poem may well be addressed to Elaine. They eventually married in 1924 but were divorced six months later, when Orr ran off to Ireland with a wealthy Irish banker, taking Nancy with her. And so it goes with the world. Cummings would not see his daughter again until 1943.

The first line of this poem, "it may not always be so," carries an echo of Rilke's:

Be ahead of all parting . . .

He was a man who, though his touch is light, always felt bound to acknowledge what is always so: everything passes. This is more commonly the realization of someone advanced in years. And yet Cummings always lived and wrote with an irrepressible youthfulness of mind and spirit. His work is threaded through with a love and delight for this remarkable world that is always passing away and, phoenixlike, renewing itself before our eyes.

Like all romantics, his two favorite subjects were love and death. His acute sense of the impermanence of things—of life, ideas, civilization—was no doubt encouraged by his experience of the First World War, and also by his turbulent love life. As well as having numerous affairs, he married three times, at last finding enduring companionship with the model and photographer Marion Morehouse, who lived with him for thirty years, until his death in 1962.

The realization that "it may not always be so" reminds me of an early conversation I had with the woman I lived with for thirteen years in England. Her name was Chloe. We could sense that our lives were going to be entwined almost as soon as we met, and yet we also knew that it would only be for a certain period of time. How long, we didn't know; but the intuition was mutual, and it was strangely awkward to acknowledge it so early on. It was why, in spite of a rich and primarily nourishing life together, we never married. And it is true that, phoenixlike, our respective lives did indeed renew themselves from the ashes of our common life.

Those ashes were the result not of some other love coming between us, as in Cummings's poem, but of a gradual parting of ways and differences of life purpose. It was more like sand slipping irrevocably through our fingers over time. In Cummings's poem, the slipping away of the lovers' bond might have been gradual, too. Or maybe it happened in an afternoon. Either way, this poem is full of tenderness for the woman he is addressing. He is reliving her touch—the feel of her lips, her hair, her hold on his heart. And yet he relives their time together with the awareness that someone else may now be enjoying the intimacy he himself once knew "in time not far away." It's almost as if, in naming one intimate moment after another, he is inoculating himself one step at a time against the pain of their parting; prising himself away, one precious memory after the other, from the embrace of their love.

Cummings was, so to speak, born into Harvard, in 1894. His father was a sociology professor, and his childhood friends were the children of other professors who lived nearby. His childhood was not only privileged; it was a loving and nourishing environment for a precocious child. His mother would read poetry to him and his sister, and encourage them to write a poem of their own every day. In a poem he wrote at the age of six, Cummings already showed signs of the unconventional style and voice that was to be his hallmark:

FATHER DEAR. BE, YOUR FATHER—
GOOD AND GOOD,

HE IS GOOD NOW, IT IS NOT GOOD TO
  SEE IT RAIN,
FATHER DEAR IS, IT, DEAR, NO FATHER
  DEAR,
LOVE, YOU DEAR,
ESTLIN.[1]

Cummings, who was always known to friends and family by his second name of Estlin, studied Classics at Harvard, where he met kindred spirits including John Dos Passos and Scofield Thayer. He volunteered as an ambulance driver in the war, and after being imprisoned in France for his outspoken antiwar convictions wrote a successful novel about his experience, *The Enormous Room.* He fell in love with Paris during his time in Europe and returned there after the war to study painting, joining the circle of Picasso and Dada and Gertrude Stein. He became a Cubist painter of some note in the twenties, and was to follow a lifelong routine of painting in the morning and writing at night. Of all the Modernists, Stein, along with Ezra Pound, was probably the greatest influence on his poetry.

At heart Cummings was a transcendentalist. He believed in the primacy of the individual, of direct insight over doctrine. His lyric and romantic form of poetry, along with his idiosyncratic, avant-garde style, was an expression of his convictions, which put him at odds with the prevailing trend toward rationalistic and formalist poetry. Later in life, he wrote that

. . . I recognize immediately three mysteries: love, art, and selftranscendence or growing.

. . . Art is a mystery; all mysteries have their source in a mystery-of-mysteries who is love: and if lovers may reach eternity directly through love herself, their mystery remains essentially that of the loving artist whose way must lie through his art, and of the loving worshipper whose aim is oneness with his god. From another point of view, every human being is in and of himself or herself illimitable; but the essence of his or of her illimitability is precisely its uniqueness—nor could all poetry (past present and future) begin to indicate the varieties of selfhood; and consequently of self transcendence.[2]

There is a solemn, heartfelt dignity that flows through this poem and holds the line against sentimentality. It is due in no small part to Cummings's use of the traditional form of the sonnet, with its fourteen lines and its "turn" in the last couplet. Although his poems are instantly recognizable for their radical punctuation, the recombination of words and phrases, his capitalization and use of the small *i*—all his avant-garde affinities—he nonetheless wrote many of his poems in the sonnet form, and had an equally strong affinity with the themes of the Romantic tradition. His experiments with poetic form were, in any event, explorations and assertions of his individuality, a core principle of Romanticism. He wrote that

it is such minutiae as commas and small "i's"
in which my . . . Firstness thrives—Firstness—
originality, individuality—elevated to a moral,
even a cosmic principle.[3]

The sonnet serves his theme here. It is the perfect me-
dium in which to couch the nobility of his gesture to his
rival:

> *if this should be, i say if this should be-*
> *you of my heart, send me a little word;*
> *that I may go unto him, and take his hands,*
> *saying, Accept all happiness from me.*

I wonder how many of us have been able to bow so
gracefully to the very person our beloved is turning
toward, even as our beloved turns away from us. I feel
humbled by these lines; by what they say of the human
being's capacity to truly love; his ability to accept the way
life moves and has its own intelligence; to bow deeply to
the reality that, in fact, we are never in control of the way
things go. I think of the ending of Mary Oliver's poem "In
Blackwater Woods," where she says that you have to be
able to do three things in order to live in this world:

> *to love what is mortal;*
> *to hold it*
>
> *against your bones knowing*
> *your own life depends on it;*

> *and, when the time comes to let it go,*
> *to let it go.*[4]

In loving what is mortal, we know that the object of our love will pass away. Even so, we love utterly, without reserve. And to let go when it is time to let go, as Cummings does here, is perhaps the final, most absolute mark of that love.

> *Then shall i turn my face, and hear one bird*
> *sing terribly afar in the lost lands.*

A heartrending cry of loss such as this would be profoundly moving in any context. It is even more moving when it follows immediately upon such a generous expression of love as the one Cummings makes here. For letting go of his beloved in the way he does, freeing her to follow her own life's deepest affections, does not mean to deny the feelings he has toward her, but on the contrary, to raise them to their subtlest and finest station. The greatest gift and expression of love is the gesture of open arms—let come what comes—not because you don't care, or because you hope to steel yourself against pain, but because you care so much that you are helpless to do anything else. You bow to what wants to happen, whatever it is. And as in these last two lines, you accept the cost, the inevitable blow to the heart. Better in this life, after all, for the heart to be broken—to take on the rich, the tender vulnerability of being human—than not.

8

ALEXANDRA LEAVING
by Leonard Cohen

Suddenly the night has grown colder.
Some deity preparing to depart.
Alexandra hoisted on his shoulder,
they slip between the sentries of your heart.

Upheld by the simplicities of pleasure,
they gain the light, they formlessly entwine;
and radiant beyond your widest measure
they fall among the voices and the wine.

It's not a trick, your senses all deceiving,
a fitful dream the morning will exhaust—
Say goodbye to Alexandra leaving.
Then say goodbye to Alexandra lost.

Even though she sleeps upon your satin.
Even though she wakes you with a kiss.
Do not say the moment was imagined.
Do not stoop to strategies like this.

As someone long prepared for this to happen,
Go firmly to the window. Drink it in.
Exquisite music. Alexandra laughing.
Your first commitments tangible again.

You who had the honour of her evening,
And by that honour had your own restored—
Say goodbye to Alexandra leaving.
Alexandra leaving with her lord.

As someone long prepared for the occasion;
In full command of every plan you wrecked—
Do not choose a coward's explanation
that hides behind the cause and the effect.

You who were bewildered by a meaning,
whose code was broken, crucifix uncrossed—
Say goodbye to Alexandra leaving.
Then say goodbye to Alexandra lost.

go firmly to the window

It doesn't always happen this way, but it is true that more than once in my life, love has swooped down, raised me up, turned my life around, and then later, flown out of the window as mysteriously and suddenly as it came. I have always felt, because of this, that love has two faces, one turned toward a specific person and the other impersonal, the face that the Greeks described so well in the figure of Eros. In his famous poem, Cohen captures wonderfully this dual nature of love.

Cohen's "Alexandra Leaving" appears in his latest book of poems, *The Book of Longing*, as well as on his CD *Ten New Songs*. It was inspired by "The God Abandons Anthony" by the Greek poet Cavafy. It warns us that as soon as some god—some force larger than our conscious mind and far beyond our conscious control—enters the human realm, we are in the territory of forces we can only bow to. We are literally in the dark, in unknown regions where magic and mystery will always have more sway than our reasonable minds.

The darkness of the god territory is a shroud that love throws over us, under which we cannot see with our normal eyes or hear with our usual ears. But as long as you feel that shroud's comfort and warmth, the belonging it inspires and the banishment of all loneliness, it is a delicious night, a darkness in which something deep within you can grow and nourish you from the inside out, whatever the future may bring.

And yes, that same delicious night will inevitably turn cold if and when love decides to leave, as Leonard Cohen warns us at the very beginning of his beautiful poem/song:

> *Suddenly the night has grown colder,*
> *Some deity preparing to depart. . . .*

Cavafy's "The God Abandons Anthony" also begins in darkness:

> *When suddenly, at midnight. . . .*[1]

I suspect that both poems begin this way because when we are alone, and especially at night, we are more receptive to the deeper currents of our life, and to the fuller implications of what it is we might be losing. In the light of day, other business presses in on us, and it is easier to forget what is rumbling below the surface as we go about our life. As Theodore Roethke says in the first line of his poem "The Taste of Self,"

> *In a dark time, the eye begins to see.*[2]

In the original poem by Cavafy, Anthony, along with Cleopatra, is losing the city of Alexandria to Hadrian, the Roman general whose army is encamped around the city walls. But Anthony is also losing the protection of his personal god, Dionysus, patron of wine, song, and ecstatic love.

In Cohen's lyric, the god of love is bearing the singer's lover, Alexandra, away on his shoulder, leaving Cohen to contemplate his fate:

they slip between the sentries of your heart.

Such a lovely image, but I'm not entirely sure whose heart he means. Perhaps it is Alexandra's own heart that has been given the slip, the god enchanting her with thoughts of better pastures, and tempting her to forget the attachment she had to Leonard Cohen—assuming it is to himself that Cohen refers as the abandoned lover in the poem (an assumption I will make in this essay). For what are the "sentries of your heart" but the attachments we develop over time for another human being? More likely, though, it is Cohen's own heart that he is referring to, his own attachment to Alexandra having been given the slip by her sudden disappearance.

Either way, the poem suggests that the personal realm of bonding to another can be trumped by an impersonal force that compels someone suddenly to change his or her mind, and for no apparent reason. Passion of this kind blows hot or cold at will without any obvious rhyme or reason. This is why there are so many stories the world over about love potions, fatal attractions, and Cupid's bow. It is why the Greeks delegated impulses like these to the gods—they come out of nowhere, and are beyond our conscious control. Love is not personal, these stories say—a difficult truth to grasp in a culture that so avidly invests in the mythos of personal, romantic love to sell anything from automobiles and vacations to roses.

Alexandra has been seduced by the pleasures of a world of light, a godly realm of radiance and wine. That she and the god of love "formlessly entwine"—that they are not embodied—suggests to me that she has been carried away by her own dreams and fantasies of a better, more exciting, more intoxicating love than the one she has left behind in the night. The fantasy of greener pastures accompanies most love stories, whether or not it ever reaches the light of day.

Whatever the reason may be, Alexandra is leaving, and Cohen reminds himself and us that this is "not a trick"; it is actually happening, however difficult it may be to believe. After all, he is in love with this woman, and he thought she was in love with him, which she was, only not now. When you have lived some years of your life with someone, or even, as in this poem, suffered the ecstasy of an exquisite evening with someone, who then simply gets up and leaves, it must be very hard to believe your eyes. After all, you may think, was your love as flimsy, as insubstantial as this? Was it all a dream, a figment of your imagination?

Yet it is true that Eros comes and goes as he pleases, no matter the bonds of attachment we may have grown over time. And when he goes, he leaves behind an emptiness; the shadow of a kind of death feels near, purpose and meaning vanish, one's life seems reduced to ashes. We become no more than a "tattered coat upon a stick," as Yeats put it. It is an existential desolation, a harrowing stage in anyone's journey. When it happens, it can seem as if our personal deity, our very life force, is abandoning us, like the wind being blown out of our lungs.

How easy it is to blame the fates, to fall into bitterness and cynicism, or to blame oneself and others for such a sorry turn of fortune. But blame is useless. It is useless, too, to mutter over your own misinformed decisions, your wrong choices, what you could have done but didn't, what you did do but should not have done.

Following the original of Cavafy's poem, Cohen bids us firmly to acknowledge the truth instead of taking comfort in blame, denial, or self-pity. Love's sudden vanishing is, after all, no fantasy,

> *a fitful dream the morning will exhaust—*
> *Say goodbye to Alexandra leaving.*
> *Then say goodbye to Alexandra lost.*

Not only is Alexandra leaving, she is gone forever; she is lost to him. The heart of this poem reveals itself in the next two verses. Cohen bids us absorb the truth as it is happening. If this very morning, your beloved was still lying by your side in bed and woke "you with a kiss," he urges us not to diminish the impact of her sudden leaving by telling yourself that the happiness you knew so recently was imaginary, that she didn't really matter so much to you anyway. This would merely be a strategy to avoid the grief of her absence.

In Cavafy's poem, a group of musicians is passing by in the street below. The musicians are a symbol of Anthony's personal deity, Dionysus, and Cavafy urges Anthony to

> *go firmly to the window*
> *and listen with deep emotion*[3]

to the "(e)xquisite music" that is passing now from his life. Listen to it with your full heart and attention, Cohen says in his version; listen to it so deeply that you feel in your bones a tangible reality again, the commitments you first made to each other in another time; a time when you felt you would be together forever.

> *You who had the honour of her evening,*
> *And by that honour had your own restored—*

This and the following stanzas are original to Cohen, and I love how rigorous he is here with the person whose lover is leaving. If you were with her even for just one evening, he says, you should consider it an honor; and an

honor that actually bestows value and honor upon you,
who were worthy of her for even that short time. It is in
that spirit that you should let her go and say goodbye
to her,

Alexandra leaving with her lord.

The lines that follow are sober indeed:

As someone long prepared for the occasion;
In full command of every plan you wrecked—

I have no idea how personal this sentiment is to Cohen's
own life but it is true that he is never slow in his poems
and songs to exercise a certain talent for self-deprecation.
The lover in this poem is long prepared for things to go
awry because he is all too aware of the many previous
occasions for happiness he has (intentionally or uninten-
tionally) sabotaged.

Cohen came to be known early in his career as the
"godfather of gloom," and there are echoes of this incli-
nation here. When I read this poem over again, it almost
feels as if the abandoned lover is being urged to let him-
self be dismembered, taken apart limb by limb by his sur-
render to the bare truth of his predicament, and even to
be grateful for it. In this way, I would call "Alexandra Leav-
ing" a deeply spiritual poem. For isn't that the essence of
any spiritual life: to embrace with humility and full aware-

ness the truth of one's experience, moment to moment? What is dismembered in moments like this is the shell of the egoic self; the one who prefers to put a good face on things; who likes to believe, if not to pretend, that he is in charge of his life and can dictate its direction at his will and leisure.

Cohen's love of women and beauty is a theme that has pervaded his work from the very beginning. As for many of us, his love has caused him to be reduced more than once to ashes in the fire of truth. Cohen's mentor in poetry was Irving Layton, the great Canadian poet who died in 2006, and Cohen's most recent poetry collection, *The Book of Longing*, from which this poem comes, is dedicated to him. Layton once said that "a poet is deeply conflicted and it is in his work that he reconciles those deep conflicts. It doesn't set the world in order, it doesn't really change anything. It is just a kind of harbor, it's the place of reconciliation, the kiss of peace." This is what I feel Cohen's poem to be, a safe harbor for those who hear in their own lives the poignant echoes of his loves and struggles; and in this case, his struggle to say an honest goodbye.

> *Do not choose a coward's explanation*
> *that hides behind the cause and the effect. . . .*

An honest goodbye is one that does not seek excuses or reasons, or explanations of any kind. Ultimately, it is not because of this or that that we part from a lover. Far from being an orderly linear progression, causes and effects form a complex web of interacting forces that together manifest in this or that result, which in its turn becomes part of the web and contributes to whatever comes next. The web itself is as broad and deep as the ocean. Behind every event, no matter how small, is a universe of causative factors stretching back through time as well as space. So let us rather bow to the fact and the mystery of what is before us, whatever it may be, and embrace its reality, regardless of its origins, without trying to control it by explaining it away.

> *You who were bewildered by a meaning,*
> *whose code was broken, crucifix uncrossed—*

The lover here, perhaps Cohen himself, could not wrap his mind around the departure of his beloved. It contravened his own moral principles, his own normative code of behavior, and even bent his spiritual code out of shape, if I understand correctly the phrase "crucifix uncrossed." Even so, the poet urges him one last time to transcend his customary ethics and standards of conduct, and to have the courage to

> *Say goodbye to Alexandra leaving.*
> *Then say goodbye to Alexandra lost.*

To have the humility, in other words, and also the strength, to acknowledge reality as it is, however much our mind and heart may be saying or screaming to us to look the other way. This, Cohen tells us in this poem, is the mark of true human dignity, and also the signature of love.

9

SONNETS TO ORPHEUS, PART TWO, XIII

by Rainer Maria Rilke

Be ahead of all parting, as if it had already happened,
like winter, which even now is passing.
For beneath the winter is a winter so endless
that to survive it at all is a triumph of the heart.

Be forever dead in Eurydice, and climb back singing.
Climb praising as you return to connection.
Here among the disappearing, in the realm of the
    transient,
be a ringing glass that shatters as it rings.

Be. And, at the same time, know what it is not to be.
That emptiness inside you
allows you to vibrate
in resonance with your world. Use it for once.

To all that has run its course, and to the vast unsayable
numbers of beings abounding in Nature,
add yourself gladly, and cancel the cost.

climb back singing

On reading the first stanza of this sonnet, you might be forgiven for thinking that Rilke was a stoic striving to steel himself against the pain and the grief of the inevitable presence of death in this world. Yet his sonnet turns out to be a glorious song of praise to the inherent mystery of life, and to the way that mystery must always, in every moment, necessarily include our mortality. In this, the sonnet he felt to be the heart of the entire Orpheus series, he gives us his deepest intuition of what he sees life's purpose to be.

The theme throughout the *Sonnets to Orpheus* is one of praise for this life and for the transformative power that can emerge in human beings when, moment by moment, they keep "life open towards death," as he put it in a letter to a friend.

> *Be ahead of all parting, as if it had already happened,*
> *like winter, which even now is passing.*
> *For beneath the winter is a winter so endless*
> *that to survive it at all is a triumph of the heart.*

Far from urging upon us the stoic philosophy of tak-
ing life's blows on the chin, that first line is instead a com-
mand to us, the reader, to feel deeply into this life as it
presents itself in this moment, which even now is passing.
Rilke is calling us to transcend our ordinary linear sense
of time, in which an event seems to emerge, have a life-
span, and to fade away. It's not like that, Rilke says. In hav-
ing an intuition of our own transience and mortality, we
realize that life exists not as a linear progression through
time at all, but as a continual flow in which all the parts of
an apparent sequence of events are present in each other
all the time. The various "stages" of our life are present all
of the time; the generations that precede us and that will
come after us are present all of the time. Life is a holo-
gram, not a three-dimensional story that ends in death. In
a letter to his Polish translator, Rilke says

> We, of this earth and this today, are not for a mo-
> ment hedged by the world of time, nor bound
> within it: we are incessantly flowing over and
> over to those who preceded us and to those who
> apparently come after us. In that widest open
> world all are.[1]

Again, in that same letter to his Polish translator:

> Death is the side of life that is turned away from
> us: we must try to achieve the fullest conscious-

ness of our existence, which is at home in the two unseparated realms, inexhaustibly nourished by both . . . The true figure of life extends through both domains, the blood of the mightiest circulation drives through both: there is neither a here nor a beyond, but the great unity. . . .[2]

To live in "the great unity" is to embrace your death in this moment's passing; to give yourself utterly to this moment, to everyone and everything it contains, "even as it turns away," he says in the twelfth sonnet.

> *Be inspired by the flame*
> *Where everything shines as it disappears.*[3]

When something disappears, as it always does, we can see its precious value more clearly than when we were standing next to it. Who has not felt an upwelling of love in waving goodbye to someone dear? Oh, to live in that love all of the time! When we live from the depth of being that can accept the parting of someone or something "in the same moment as we love them more than our heart can bear," then we open ourselves to multiple dimensions of being; to the intuition of a winter beneath all winters, a darkness beyond all knowing of darkness.

Just as there can be a dream within a dream, whereby even the notion of a dreamer itself becomes fluid—so, too, our notion of our waking self, with its story of a personal life from birth to death, is called into question when we start to become aware of transient reality.

"Transience everywhere plunges us into a deep being," Rilke says. The awareness of our passing and the continual passing of all things enables us to wake up into the preciousness of the moment we are living—not as a concept, but as a living experience that runs like a fine current through every cell. With this awareness, death is not something that ends life; it is present in life throughout. It is a lived reality that joins us to all living things and imbues all existence with vitality and fullness.

Rilke's *Sonnets to Orpheus* are generally considered to be his greatest work, and, appropriately, they came about in a mysterious way. Before the First World War, Rilke had begun what he felt would be his most inspired work, the *Duino Elegies,* but during the war he found it increasingly difficult to write, and only in 1921 did he find the peace of mind and also the place where the muse could speak to him again. In that year, funded by wealthy friends, Rilke moved to the thirteenth-century Chateau de Muzot in Switzerland. For months Rilke wrote nothing but correspondence, and a lot of it.

Then, in a life-changing moment of serendipity, his lover at the time, Baladine Klossowska, left a postcard pinned above his desk, then withdrew. It showed Orpheus under a tree with his lyre, singing to the animals. Early in 1922, apparently out of nowhere, a great wave of poetry surged up within him and poured onto the page in the form of a series of sonnets to Orpheus. In just over two weeks, fifty-five poems arrived complete, in the standard sonnet form of fourteen lines with end rhymes. They arrived with an astonishing speed and fluidity that seemed to suggest they had been dictated to him rather than having been composed. In between the sonnets, he also wrote the seventh, the eighth, the ninth, and the tenth *Duino Elegies,* completing that series as well.

In this sonnet, Rilke is shaking up the very notion of who we think we are. His poems were never, after all, intended merely for the rational mind. As he himself said, the sonnets are rather to be grasped in a moment of inspiration on the part of the reader, not "with what is called 'understanding.' "[4]

> *Be forever dead in Eurydice, and climb back singing.*
> *Climb praising as you return to connection.*

The god and poet Orpheus went down into the Underworld to retrieve his beloved Eurydice, who had been killed by a snake bite. He enchanted Hades, the ruler, with his music, and persuaded him to allow Eurydice to return with him to earth. Hades agreed on condition that Orpheus not turn to look at his beloved on the journey, though he did, of course, just before reaching the light. His punishment was to be torn to shreds by the Maenads, the female worshippers of Dionysus. They threw his head into the river Hebrus, and it floated, still singing, down to the sea.

This last image was an inspiration for Rilke, who insists

through all his work that the poet be a praising person; that whatever his fate, his song is all and will not perish. The other motif in the Orpheus myth is the omnipresence of the world of Hades, and in telling the reader in this sonnet to be "forever dead in Eurydice," Rilke is urging us to be like Orpheus; to live like him in a "double realm," one in which we can know and feel the moment we are living to be passing even as we taste it to the full. This is the twofold knowing that brings truth to existence. Without that truth, we live in a dream everlasting, as if we were immortal. Then, as Shakespeare says in *The Tempest*,

> *We are such stuff*
> *As dreams are made on, and our little life*
> *Is rounded with a sleep.*[5]

To Rilke's mind, that is not really living at all. We are sleepwalking through life when we live as if death were not on our shoulder. The theme of waking up from the fantasy of immortality is a vein that runs through all of Rilke's work. When, like Orpheus, we have seen through that fantasy, we can "climb back singing."

Then our song will keep on ringing out whether we are alive or dead, like the head of Orpheus singing as it floats down the river. Surely this is what Rilke means when he says

> *Here among the disappearing, in the realm of the transient,*
> *be a ringing glass that shatters as it rings.*

We are "the disappearing." Everyone alive today, whatever their age, is shuffling in one great community, one endless procession, toward the farther shore. Death is perfectly safe. Nobody fails to cross over. Knowing this in our heart and mind, what else is there to do but throw up our arms and sing? Shattering even as we ring.

> *Be. And, at the same time, know what it is not to be.*
> *That emptiness inside you*
> *allows you to vibrate*
> *in resonance with your world. Use it for once.*

Another word for Orpheus's song—for Rilke's death-in-life—is *emptiness.* Not being. But emptiness is not always so transcendent. I have known an emptiness that can turn my days to ashes. On days like that I am a boat without a rudder, adrift in a fog of inertia. Everything is gray, absent any luster of meaning. Life is not worth living.

But sometimes, if a glimmer of attention, a sliver of curiosity, remains to me, then I can take that little light deeper into the blackness and feel, not think, what it is that ails me. Those are the times when I can plunge into a deeper, even blacker emptiness that is not really emptiness at all but a vastness—a spaciousness, a vibrant spaciousness that allows me to expand beyond notions of meaning and meaningless altogether. To expand into being itself. It is this that allows me to "vibrate in resonance" with my world again.

This full emptiness is the source of life itself; of all true inspiration, of art, poetry, and love. The character Charles Citrine in Saul Bellow's novel *Humboldt's Gift* reflects on it eloquently while on a flight to New York:

> Once in a while, I get shocked into upper wakefulness, I turn a corner, see the ocean, and my heart tips over with happiness—it feels so free! Then I have the idea that, as well as beholding, I can also be beheld from yonder and am not a discrete object but incorporated with the rest, with universal sapphire, purplish blue. For what is this sea, this atmosphere, doing within the eight-inch diameter of your skull? (I say nothing of the sun and the galaxy which are also there.) At the very center of the beholder there must be space for the whole, and this nothing-space is not an empty nothing but a nothing reserved for everything. You can feel this nothing-everything capacity with ecstasy, and this is what I actually felt in the jet. Sipping whisky, feeling the radiant heat that rose inside, I experienced a bliss that I knew perfectly well was not mad.[6]

Charles Citrine is "vibrating in resonance" with the world. Saul Bellow is writing his novel on the wings of that ecstasy, the ecstasy of Orpheus. He is doing what Rilke urges us to do:

Use it for once.

There is only one Saul Bellow, only one Rilke; the question for us is how we might use or express that full emptiness of being—our own Orphic song—in our own way in our own life. This is what joins us with the great chorus and choir of all things—to

the vast unsayable
numbers of beings abounding in Nature, . . .

Finally, in pondering the nature of our own song, we might benefit from the advice Rilke gives in one of his *Letters to a Young Poet,* when he says

> I would like to beg you dear Sir, as well as I can,
> to have patience with everything unresolved in
> your heart and to try to love the questions them-
> selves as if they were locked rooms or books
> written in a very foreign language. Don't search
> for the answers, which could not be given to
> you now, because you would not be able to live
> them. And the point is to live everything. Live
> the questions now. Perhaps then, someday far in
> the future, you will gradually, without even no-
> ticing it, live your way into the answer.[7]

10

WHEN YOUR LIFE LOOKS BACK
by Jane Hirshfield

When your life looks back—
as it will, at itself, at you—what will it say?

Inch of colored ribbon cut from the spool.
Flame curl, blue-consuming the log it flares from.
Bay leaf. Oak leaf. Cricket. One among many.

Your life will carry you as it did always,
with ten fingers and both palms,
with horizontal ribs and upright spine,
with its filling and emptying heart,
that wanted only your own heart, emptying, filled,
*   in return.*
You gave it. What else could you do?

Immersed in air or in water.
Immersed in hunger or anger.
Curious even when bored.
Longing even when running away.

"What will happen next?"—
the question hinged in your knees, your ankles,
in the in-breaths even of weeping.

Strongest of magnets, the future impartial drew you in.
Whatever direction you turned toward was face to face.
No back of the world existed,
no unseen corner, no test. No other earth to prepare for.

This, *your life had said, its only pronoun.*
Here, *your life had said, its only house.*
Let, *your life had said, its only order.*

And did you have a choice in this? You did—

Sleeping and waking,
The horses around you, the mountains around you,
The buildings with their tall, hydraulic shafts.
Those of your own kind around you—

A few times, you stood on your head.
A few times, you chose not to be frightened.
A few times, you found yourself held beyond any
    measure.

Mortal, *your life will say,*
As if tasting something delicious, as if in envy.
Your immortal life will say this, as it is leaving.

your immortal life will say this

I sit here looking out over an expanse of blue water. Berkeley and San Francisco rim the horizon; the sleekness of the Bay Bridge stretches between them. This is where my life has brought me; from across another ocean, another land, another people, to this window with a ferry boat gliding by. In that other land I knew, in that other time I knew, far away and long ago, in the distant pictures of my childhood, that ferry would have steamed its way through choppier, grayer waters. Plumes of gray-black smoke would have drifted from a funnel grimy with use. Between then and now, between waters gray and blue has stretched my life; and I can feel again, on reading this poem—and I say this in wonder, rather than in sadness—how it, too, is one more trace of smoke curling on the wind.

> *When your life looks back—*
> *as it will, at itself, at you—what will it say?*

This is a deeply kind and compassionate poem; and one that has not been published before. Jane Hirshfield is not of the materialist Richard Dawkins school; the "when you are dead you are dead" school. She is a Buddhist, and yet while Buddhists generally avoid all talk of the soul, Hirshfield supposes in her very first line that at death there will be something that endures and that gazes with compassion at your story from a certain distance. Even so, true to her Buddhist background, she avoids the term *soul* and its tendency to imply something solid, a *thing*, from what is ultimately a mystery. This also allows her to skip over the implicit duality of the pairing, body and soul.

What will our "life" say of us, she asks, as it looks back, "at itself, at you"? These two are not different—not separate entities, she wants us to know. And yet, and yet. She forges a crucial sense of perspective in these first lines. She encourages a distinction of sorts between our life story and our life; between what I take to be self-consciousness (our ego) and our essence (the ground, the field of awareness within which our ego story unfolds).

When I read these lines I am struck by how little I know myself from this other perspective of awareness that, for the convenience of clarity—and because I am more permeated with Western than with Buddhist thought—I will call here the soul; how rarely I have slipped out of my own story and seen it and felt it from the soul's perspective. How can the fish know what water is? The very air I breathe I normally breathe as Roger Housden. I drink in and fortify Roger with every breath, with every good or doubtful intention, every thought and feeling, every book, every relationship, every move of house or country; with every story I tell. All of it goes to feed the notion of who I think I am.

And yet if we were fish, we would be flying fish. We have the capacity to live in two worlds. What, then, does our life look like when we have slipped out of our habitual self and can see with the eyes of the soul?

> Inch of colored ribbon cut from the spool.
> Flame curl, blue-consuming the log it flares from.
> Bay leaf. Oak leaf. Cricket. One among many.

A sliver of ribbon from the great spool of life. A brief flash of fire that feeds on the log of the body and the sense-world; that same body that binds it for a while to the earth. Only the voice of the soul, which lives on the edge of the personal and the impersonal, would put it like this. What would the voice of "your" soul say? We are one among many, Hirshfield says. Just like the bay leaf or the cricket. One among many. With the dawning of this realization comes a precious gift. Czeslaw Milosz's poem "Love" begins with these lines:

> *Love means to look at yourself*
> *The way one looks at distant things*
> *For you are only one thing among many.*[1]

The gift of seeing like this, his poem goes on to say, is a heart healed "from various ills." The natural world will

look upon us as a friend, as one of its own. To see our-
selves from a certain distance, as only the soul can do, is to
see how we share the same mortal fate as all living things.
It is to feel love for our own passing story and the passing
story of all things. This is the heart of Jane's poem.

Your life animates the body through all its cells, and is
not separate from it. The body with its "horizontal ribs
and upright spine" is what keeps your story moving. Your
life, Hirshfield says,

> . . . *wanted only your own heart, emptying, filled,*
>   *in return.*

I am reminded of these few lines from "Love After
Love," a poem by Derek Walcott:

> *Give back your heart*
> *To itself, to the stranger who has loved you*
> *All your life, whom you ignored*
> *For another, who knows you by heart.*[2]

The stranger here, the one who loves you and "knows
you by heart," is the soul itself, whose desires are so eas-
ily ignored for the wants and urgencies of the ego and its
compelling story. The soul, "your life," who loves you, de-
sires the fullness of your heart. Of course it does. To be
wholehearted is to be fully engaged with your life. Who is
it then that is

> *Curious even when bored.*
> *Longing even when running away?*

Who is it that asks,

> *"What will happen next?"*

To my ears it is the soul who is curious and who continues to long for something, something without a name, even as your body is turning the other way. We might assume it to be the ego who always wants to know what's next, and perhaps we would be right. Yet maybe the soul, too, is curious about the storyline; not in an anxious, but in an interested way, like someone reading a novel.

Your life's attention, though, is most naturally at home on the page of the present, in what is happening now.

> This, *your life had said, its only pronoun.*
> Here, *your life had said, its only house.*
> Let, *your life had said, its only order.*

In another of her poems, Hirshfield says

> *Your story was this: you were happy, then you were sad,*
> *You slept, you awakened.*
> *Sometimes you ate roasted chestnuts, sometimes*
>   *persimmons.*[3]

Others may have all sorts of things to say about you, but they will miss the obvious, the chestnuts and the persimmons. They will miss your succession of present moments. How easy it is to become immersed and enmeshed in dramatic events, in apparently life-changing turns of fate. And yet all the while, we are breathing; or rather, life is breathing us. All the while, our hand, without thinking, brings some fruit to our lips and we bite into its succulent flesh. We sit down, we stand up, we go outside, we lie on the bed with our beloved, we walk alone, and possibly lonely, beneath the shade of the spreading elms. This is our life, lived moment by moment, even as our feverish brain generates wonderful or dismal futures, or regurgitates the dreams and losses of the past. We go on living, no matter what, until we don't.

And did you have a choice in this? You did—

The choice we have, I believe, is not so much about one action over another, whether to go or stay, to do this or that, but rather whether our awareness is lost in daydreams or simply looking on, curious, "the way one looks at distant things. . . ." Only then can we choose "not to be frightened"; because with that compassionate distance, we are no longer immersed in the fear. In such a moment, the fear is a wave on the sea of our awareness.

Angels, I imagine, know neither fear nor love, being beyond the grip of the personal. Their love would be of the transcendent, transpersonal kind; the love of all beings, the infinite compassion of a Bodhisattva. It is the same for our "immortal life," which is of the angels, and free of the vagaries of our personal self.

> Mortal, *your life will say,*
> *As if tasting something delicious, as if in envy.*
> *Your immortal life will say this, as it is leaving.*

That's it! That's the wondrous gift of being human! We alone, of all beings visible and invisible, can live in two worlds at once. In this poem, Hirshfield manages a lovely thing; she gives equal value to our mortal and immortal selves. In her world, one is not superior to the other. Body and spirit together are required to forge something unique, a third thing, the human soul, which is both of this world and not of it at the same time.

Our story, our life of the senses and feelings and thoughts, it all matters after all. It is precisely what our "immortal life" can never experience, and, if it only had feelings, might be envious of. It can never know what it is like to hold another "beyond any measure," or to find "yourself held beyond any measure." Our personal life and story is something *delicious,* and in this poem, our immortal life bids it the most loving farewell, implying that we, too, would do well to love our life, whatever shape it is in, while we still have it.

Our own curl of smoke on the wind is, paradoxically, our gateway to freedom. For only here, in this beautiful, fragile, and disappearing body, can we know the meaning of love. All the more reason, then, to ponder the question—to "live" the question, Rilke would say—of how best to live your "one wild and precious life"[4]—today, and today, and today, while your heart is still beating.

about the poets

ELLEN BASS (b.1947)

Billy Collins has said of Ellen Bass's work that her "frighteningly personal poems about sex, love, birth, motherhood, and aging are kept from mere confession by the graces of wit, an observant eye, an empathetic heart, and just the right image deployed at just the right time." Bass is the author of several nonfiction books, including *The Courage to Heal,* which has been translated into nine languages. Her poetry volume *Mules of Love* (BOA, 2002) won the Lambda Literary Award, and she has also won the Pushcart Prize and the Pablo Neruda Prize for poetry. Her most recent collection, *The Human Line,* came out with Copper Canyon Press in 2007. Bass teaches in the low-residency MFA Program at Pacific University, and has taught poetry and creative writing in Santa Cruz, California.

LEONARD COHEN (b. 1934)

Leonard Cohen was born in Montreal, Canada. His artistic career began in 1956 with the publication of his first book of poetry, *Let Us Compare Mythologies,* which was reissued by Ecco in a fiftieth-anniversary edition. Cohen is the author of twelve books, including two novels—*The Favorite Game* and *Beautiful Losers*—and the recent collection of poems and songs, *Stranger Music.* He has made seventeen albums. His haunting songs have left their mark on a generation who came of age in the sixties and seventies. Internationally celebrated for both his writing and his music, Cohen is one of the great legendary performers and artists of our time. His *Book of Longing,* finally completed after his time as a monk in Mt. Baldy Zen Center outside Los Angeles, is an inspired collection of poetry and line drawings.

e. e. cummings (1894–1962)

Cummings was born in Cambridge, Massachussetts. In his poetry he experimented radically with form, punctuation, spelling, and syntax, creating a new, highly personal means of poetic expression. At Harvard, he delivered a daring commencement address on Modernist artistic innovations, thus announcing the direction his work would take. Love poems, satirical poems, and descriptive nature poems were his favored forms. At the time of his death he was the second most widely read poet in the United States, after Robert Frost.

JACK GILBERT (b. 1925)

Jack Gilbert, born in Pittsburgh, was educated both in his hometown and in San Francisco. Soon after publishing his first book of poems, in 1962, he went on a Guggenheim Fellowship to Europe, where he stayed for many years, mostly in Greece. *Monolithos,* his second volume, was published twenty years after his first. Gilbert has always remained firm in his avoidance of the beaten path to success and recognition, preferring the authenticity of a life on a remote Greek island to the ambitions in New York City. The poet James Dickey once said, "He takes himself away to a place more inward than it is safe to go; from that awful silence and tightening, he returns to us poems of savage compassion." Gilbert's *Refusing Heaven,* published in 2005, won the National Book Critics Circle Award.

ROBERT HAYDEN (1913–1980)

Robert Hayden was raised by foster parents in a poor neighborhood of Detroit. His poor eyesight prevented him from playing sports, which gave him the time and inclination to read literature. With the help of a scholarship, he attended Detroit City College in 1932. His first book of poems, *Heart-Shape in the Dust,* was published in 1940. He enrolled in a graduate English literature program where he was mentored by W. H. Auden. He had an interest in African American history and explored in his poetry issues of race. Michael S. Harper has said that Hayden is "a real testament to craft, to vision, to complexity and historical consciousness, and to love and transcendence." Passionately committed to the discipline and craft of poetry, Hayden was the first African American to hold the position of American poet laureate. He died in Ann Arbor, Michigan, in 1980.

JANE HIRSHFIELD (b. 1953)

Hirshfield is a prize-winning poet, translator, editor, and author of six collections of poetry. Born in New York City, she received her BA at Princeton in the first graduating class to accept women. She went to San Francisco and was a full-time practitioner at the Zen Center there for many years. Her collection *Given Sugar, Given Salt* was a finalist for the National Book Critics Circle Award in 2001. Her work addresses the life of the passions, the way the objects and events of everyday life are informed by deeper wisdoms and by the darkness and losses of life. Her poetry searches continually for the point where new knowledge of the world and self may appear, and carries the influence of her lifelong study and practice of Buddhism. Her most recent collection in the United States is *After*, published by HarperCollins in 2007.

DORIANNE LAUX (b. 1952)

Laux has an Irish, French, and Algonquin heritage, and she grew up in Maine. Between the ages of eighteen and thirty, she worked as a gas station manager, sanatorium cook, maid, and doughnut holer. A single mother, she took occasional poetry classes at a local junior college, writing poems during shift breaks. In 1983 she moved to Berkeley and began writing in earnest. Supported by scholarships and grants, she returned to school and graduated in 1988 with a degree in English. She has won various awards and has published three collections of poetry. In *The Gettysburg Review*, Tony Hoagland writes that "Laux is a believer in desire, and she takes her stance as a hero of the ordinary, with both feet planted firmly in the luminous material world."

PABLO NERUDA (1904–1973)

Pablo Neruda is widely seen as the most important Latin American poet of the twentieth century, as well as an influential contributor to major developments in modern poetry. He was born in the provincial town of Parral, in Chile, the son of a teacher and a railway worker. He moved to the capital, Santiago, for his university education and published his first poetry collection, *Crepusculario*, in 1923 at the age of nineteen. *Twenty Love Poems and a Song of Despair*, which has since been translated into dozens of languages, came out the following year. Between 1927 and 1935 he held a series of honorary consulships around the world, and in 1934 he returned to Chile, soon to become a senator of the Republic and a member of the Communist Party of Chile. His political interests strongly colored the poetic output of his middle years, though his complete oeuvre, running to several thousand pages, spans a vast range of ideas and passions. He received the Nobel Prize in Literature in 1971.

RAINER MARIA RILKE (1875–1926)

Rilke survived a lonely and unhappy childhood in Prague to publish his first volume of poetry, *Leben und Lieder,* in 1894. He left Prague in 1896 for the University of Munich. He later traveled to Italy, then Russia. In 1902 in Paris he became friend and secretary to the sculptor Rodin, and the next twelve years there saw his greatest poetic activity. In 1919 he moved to Switzerland, where he wrote his last two works, *Sonnets to Orpheus* and *Duino Elegies,* in 1923. He died in Switzerland of leukemia in 1926. His reputation has grown enormously since his death, and he is now considered one of the greatest poets of the twentieth century.

GERALD STERN (b. 1925)

Stern was born to immigrant parents in Pittsburgh. He has written poetry all his life, though his first book was not published until he was forty-eight. He claims to have "come from nowhere, and never had any mentors." He has spent his life as a poet and teacher, having held posts at several American universities. Since his first volume, which received great critical acclaim, he has gone on to publish more than thirteen books, to receive many awards, and to be the first poet laureate of New Jersey. William Matthews has said that Stern is "a poet of ferocious heart and rasping sweetness." Like Whitman, his work is a transformational celebration of the stuff of daily existence.

notes

INTRODUCTION

1. Excerpt from C. P. Cavafy, "The God Abandons Anthony," *C. P. Cavafy: Selected Poems,* translated by Edmund Keeley and Philip Sherrard (Princeton, NJ: Princeton University Press, 1972).

1. IF YOU KNEW

1. Excerpt from Ellen Bass, "Basket of Figs," *Mules of Love* (Rochester, NY: BOA Editions, 2002).
2. Excerpt from Ellen Bass, "The Moon," Ibid.
3. Excerpt from Antonio Machado, "Last Night as I Lay Sleeping," *Times Alone: Selected Poems of Antonio Machado,* trans. Robert Bly (Middletown, CT: Wesleyan University Press, 1983).
4. Excerpt from Czeslaw Milosz, "Encounter," *New and Collected Poems: 1931–2001* (New York: Ecco Press, 2003).

2. LOVE SONNET XCIV

1. Excerpt from Dylan Thomas, "Do Not Go Gentle," *The Poems of Dylan Thomas, New Revised Edition* (New York: New Directions, 2003).
2. Excerpt from Pablo Neruda, "Love Sonnet LIX," *100 Love Sonnets,* translated by Stephen Tapscott (Austin: University of Texas Press, 1959).

3. HOW IT WILL HAPPEN, WHEN

1. From Dorianne Laux, "Abschied's Symphony," *Smoke* (Rochester, NY: BOA Editions, 2000).
2. Excerpt from Dorianne Laux and Kim Addonizio, *The Poet's Companion* (New York: Norton, 1997).
3. Excerpt from Kahlil Gibran, "On Pain," *The Prophet* (www.bnpublishing.net: BN Publishing, 2006).
4. Excerpt from David Whyte, "The Well of Grief," *Where Many Rivers Meet* (Langley, WA: Many Rivers Press, 1990).

4. THE LOST HOTELS OF PARIS

1. Excerpt from Jack Gilbert, "A Kind of Courage," *Refusing Heaven* (New York: Knopf, 2007).
2. Excerpt from Jack Gilbert, "Happening Apart from What's Happening Around It," Ibid.
3. Excerpt from "Meanwhile," Ibid.
4. Excerpt from "The Mistake," Ibid.

5. WAVING GOOD-BYE

1. Excerpt from Gerald Stern, "The Red Coal," *This Time: New and Selected Poems of Gerald Stern* (New York: Norton, 1999).
2. Excerpt from Gerald Stern, "The Dancing," Ibid.
3. Excerpt from Rumi, "Last Night a Man Was Crying," *The Essential Rumi,* translated by Coleman Barks (San Francisco: Harper, 1995).

6. THOSE WINTER SUNDAYS

1. From Sherry Anderson, "Not Remembering the Beginning," unpublished poem, with permission of the author.

2. From Philip Larkin, "An Arundel Tomb," *Selected Poems* (New York: Farrar, Straus and Giroux, 2007).

7. it may not always be so; and i say

1. From e. e. cummings, "i and now and him," *Nonlecture V, Six Nonlectures* (Cambridge: Harvard University Press, 1953).
2. Ibid.
3. From Christopher Sawyer-Laucanno, *E. E. Cummings: A Biography* (Naperville, IL: Sourcebooks, 2004), p. 168.
4. From Mary Oliver, "In Blackwater Woods," *New and Selected Poems* (Boston: Beacon Press, 1994).

8. ALEXANDRA LEAVING

1. From C. P. Cavafy, "The God Abandons Anthony," *C. P. Cavafy: Collected Poems,* translated by Edmund Keeley and Philip Sherrard (Princeton, NJ: Princeton University Press, 1992).
2. From Theodore Roethke, "The Taste of Self," *The Collected Poems of Theodore Roethke* (New York: Anchor Books, 1995).
3. From C. P. Cavafy, "The God Abandons Anthony."

9. SONNETS TO ORPHEUS, PART TWO, XIII

1. From Rilke's letter to his Polish translator, quoted in the Introduction to *The Notebooks of Malte Laurids Brigge,* translated by Burton Pike (Champaign, IL: Dalkey Archive Press, 2008).
2. Ibid.
3. From Rainer Maria Rilke, "Sonnets to Orpheus XII," *In Praise of Mortality,* translated by Anita Barrows and Joanna Macey (New York: Riverhead Books, 2005).

4. From Rilke's letter to an unnamed Swiss friend, quoted in *Sonnets to Orpheus,* translated by M. D. Herter Norton (New York: Norton, 2006).

5. From William Shakespeare, *The Tempest,* act 4, scene 1, li. 149–58.

6. Excerpt from Saul Bellow, *Humboldt's Gift* (New York: Penguin Books, 1973).

7. Excerpt from Rainer Maria Rilke, *Letters to a Young Poet,* translated by Stephen Mitchell (www.bnpublishing.net: BN Publishing, 2009).

10. WHEN YOUR LIFE LOOKS BACK

1. Excerpt from Czeslaw Milosz, "Love," *The Collected Poems, 1931–1987* (New York: Ecco Press, 1992).

2. Excerpt from Derek Walcott, "Love After Love," *Collected Poems 1948–1984* (New York: Farrar, Straus and Giroux, 1986).

3. From Jane Hirshfield, "It Was Like This: You Were Happy," *After* (New York: Harper Perennial, 2007).

4. From Mary Oliver "A Summer Day," *New and Selected Poems* (Boston: Beacon Press, 1994).

acknowledgments

First and foremost I want to thank those poets whose work I have used to illustrate the theme of this book. Without their poems, the book would not exist. Then, my gratitude goes to Kate Kennedy, my editor, who shepherded this book through the byzantine processes of publishing to reach its final form. And once again, my heartfelt thanks go to my agent, Joy Harris.

permissions

about the author

ROGER HOUSDEN is the author of some twenty books, including the bestselling Ten Poems series, three travel books, and the novella *Chasing Rumi*. He is also a writing coach, and leads occasional literary and art appreciation journeys. You can find out more on www.rogerhousden.com.